PRAISE FOR
YOU ARE YOUR DESIRES

"You are your desires" is a wonderfully written, life affirming book that will inspire everybody to experience their unique and authentic self with courage and conviction. What makes this book so profound is its honesty without even a trace of superficial sermonizing. Thus, it encourages the reader to seek and shape their unique destiny. At 92 years of age, after reading this book, I was able to look back on my life and relate the play of desire, will and action in my personal and professional life. This is an eye-opening book that will change how we think about desires and destiny.

Singeetam Srinivasa Rao
is an internationally renowned award winning Film Director, Writer and Producer.

* * *

With a firm foundation in Indian tradition, Anita Vallabh offers a refreshing perspective on an ancient wisdom template in a relatable and enjoyable manner. In this motivational book, she delves into her vast experience and those of her friends and family to relate the play of desire, will, and action in shaping one's destiny. She beautifully interweaves philosophy to everyday living in an easily readable and very enjoyable manner. It is an essential read for anybody, anywhere in the world who wants to make choices aligned to their personality and be happier at work and at home.

Dr Sharda Narayanan,
Author and Assistant Professor,
Dr MGR Janaki College of
Arts & Science for Women, Chennai.

* * *

"You are Your Desires" includes a rich collection of stories that bring jewels of wisdom to light. Anita Vallabh's style is a call to the heart that explores the great potential within each individual to shape destiny. This book is for anyone who is soul searching and cultivates a focus on awareness and intention-making that guides the reader to hidden treasures through imagination. Thoughtful and thorough, it's a wonderful read that creates a vision for joyfulness.

Dr. Kara Jhalak Miller
Professor of Dance,
University of Hawai'i at Mānoa

* * *

A great guide to traversing our jungle of emotions, desires, values, behaviors and actions over time, and helping us articulate what it is we truly want. I really enjoyed reading this informative book.

Suriya Gangen,
Founder of The Suriya Project (Souht Africa),
Valuation & Risk Consultant (South Africa).

* * *

YOU ARE YOUR DESIRES

HOW AN ANCIENT INDIAN
WISDOM TEMPLATE WILL HELP YOU
TAP INTO YOUR DESIRES AND SHAPE YOUR
HIGHEST DESTINY.

ANITA VALLABH Ph.D

INDIA • SINGAPORE • MALAYSIA

Copyright © Anita Vallabh 2024
All Rights Reserved.

ISBN
Paperback 979-8-89002-967-6
Hardcase 979-8-89277-786-5

This book has been published with all efforts taken to make the material error-free after the consent of the author. However, the author and the publisher do not assume and hereby disclaim any liability to any party for any loss, damage, or disruption caused by errors or omissions, whether such errors or omissions result from negligence, accident, or any other cause.

While every effort has been made to avoid any mistake or omission, this publication is being sold on the condition and understanding that neither the author nor the publishers or printers would be liable in any manner to any person by reason of any mistake or omission in this publication or for any action taken or omitted to be taken or advice rendered or accepted on the basis of this work. For any defect in printing or binding the publishers will be liable only to replace the defective copy by another copy of this work then available.

"…discovery of the sages binds the whole of humanity in the harmony of the cosmos…"

Swami Rama
Living with the Himalayan Masters

I offer my salutations to the Seers
Who see, and who know.

To those who have crossed the turbulent ocean of life,
To the shore of bliss,
From whence they help seekers across,
By sharing pearls of wisdom.

For the love, compassion and deep knowing,
Of the immense potential of humankind,
To reach the shore and mark its footprint,
Along the sands of time.

I dedicate this book to my beloved grandmother Sitarama,
and father Dakshina Murthy:
the brightest stars that guide me from a place far and above
where they enjoy the best seats to the play of life.

CONTENTS

PART 1. GOING INWARD

PART 2. ĀRṢA DHARMA, THE WISDOM OF SEERS

THE DESIRE MANIFESTO

The seers explored wide and deep
To bring back secrets of life and living.
They recognized that Desire,
The all-too-powerful impulse
That created our world,
Rests within us.

From the sacred space of the 'heart'
It calls to us in whispers:
An urge, an idea, a desire.
To express and experience.

The timeless wisdom of the heart,
Calling and seeking to be expressed.
In honoring the Call,
In unlocking and integrating Its wisdom in our choices,
Problems become challenges, obstacles guide our way and,
Hardships become explorations.

In its unfolding Grace and beauty
We come to stand for the best and brightest in us.

We thus honor life;
We honor our empowering, sacred Soul energy.

– Anita Vallabh

GRATITUDE

It has been an incredible blessing to have spent the last eight years on this project, thinking, reminiscing and staying curious.

This book would not have been possible if not for the courage shown by my dear friends Shari, Sanjay Chaganti, Suchint Murali, Susan Pokorney, and my father-in-law Sriramulu Vallabhajyosula in sharing their stories. I am grateful for their unquestioning trust in my ability to steward the flow of desire in their lives.

I am indebted to my Guru Dr. Pappu Venugopala Rao. He inspires me to delve deep into every Sanskrit phrase and seek its multifaceted meaning. As did my brilliant friend Suyasha Sengupta to whom I turned every so often for counsel concerning Vedic philosophy. I thank her for her generosity in sharing her immense knowledge.

I express my gratitude to the students who attended my workshops on desire in Chennai. Their responses helped shape the 'zoom-in' questions in this book.

Many authors were with me in spirit and to them I owe a great debt of gratitude. They gave me the language and courage to write and fulfill my heartfelt desire. I am listing only a few of them here due to space constraints. In no way does this very short list make less the contribution of other teachers and writers who show up every day to leave their signature in the literary world.

To the spirit of Eknath Easwaran, whose loving relationship with his grandmother recalled my own. His writings on "The Essence of Upanishads and the Bhagavad Gita" showed me how complex ideas can become simple, fun practices. His writings were the beacon that guided the path to this book.

To the spiritual head of the Himalayan Institute at Honesdale, Pennsylvania, Pundit Tigunait as well as my teachers Shari Friedrichsen and Rolf Sovik for living by the wisdom of seers.

Brené Brown for writing Gifts of Imperfection, Daring Greatly and articulating what it means to be vulnerable and live wholeheartedly. It is because of her I now wear my imperfections like haute couture and dare greatly. If not for her work I, as an Indian American would never have had the gumption to begin the book by talking about my divorce, considered a shame in my culture.

To Elizabeth Gilbert whose TED talks and writings (particularly Big Magic) stoke my creative fire. Taking her cue, I cultivated the practice of moving my fears from the driver's seat to the back seat, giving them no power in decision-making while my creative self drove this book to its completion.

My most trusted friend Madhu Krishna for making the ordinary, endearingly special with his design inputs.

To Shannon Sexton and Poonam Ganglani for reading the first draft and giving their no-nonsense, yet kind, editorial suggestions that shaped the interiors of this book.

To the team at Notion Press, Rohan Reddy (Publishing Consultant), Kavya Reddy (Publishing Manager), Mangala (Editor), Sathish Kumar (Interior Designer), Francis (Cover Designer) and Vinoth K (Quality Check), I owe a debt of thanks for their attention to detail and support through the challenging process of completing this book.

To my lovely grandmother Sitarama whose very mention lights me up, and my mother Aruna Murthy for passing on the artistic gene and dealing with the worst of me in the best way possible.

To my uncle Narasimhan, whose saint-like virtues fill me with hope and never fail to inspire.

To my husband Sagar, witness to my temperaments (artistic, I insist), co-passenger in my creative journey, my heart and my one true love.

I thank you, my reader. For whatever reasons you hold this book in your hands, consider its contents a personal message written thousands of years ago, rewritten, and delivered to you by me.

PART 1

. . . .

GOING INWARD

O Kāma, with whatever wish we make this
offering to thee,
May it be all fulfilled for us[1].

. . . .

[1] Atharva veda, Book 19, hymn 52.5.

INTRODUCTION: YOU ARE YOUR DESIRES

I will start by addressing desires in a concrete and relatable way. To be more specific, I will begin with how I came to experience and later acknowledge the power of desires in my life. I do this by sharing with you openly and directly a difficult time in my life; a time, I can now look back on with gratitude for its many teachable experiences.

Here it is.

In 2006 I lost two men I loved; my father passed away and my husband left me for another woman. I couldn't articulate, or give some form to the depth and nuance of this devastating experience. I remember feeling lost in what seemed an unending vortex of pain, loneliness, and self-loathing.

As I was lying on my bed crying, from somewhere deep within the folds of despair a thought, rather a question, arose: What would I want my six-year-old daughter to do, were she to be in my place? That thought was to be a defining inflection point in my life.

The choices I made from then on—leaving Bangkok, going back home to India, filing for divorce, starting an art school, believing, trusting, and falling in love again, and leading a profoundly fulfilling life—evolved as an answer to that question. At every step, I acted on what I thought was good for my daughter.

Should I be running around lawyers and courts or should I spend more time with her? I spent more time with her.

I asked myself, What did I want for her?

Should I live in perpetual anguish over money or should I start looking for a job? I started looking for jobs.

Should I continue to have a relationship with his family and listen to recurring conversations of the 'could haves' and 'should haves'? I broke away completely (no half-measures for me) and started anew.

So many questions, so many decisions to be made and choices to be acted upon. There were potholes to circumvent, hurdles to cross accompanied by constant self-doubt (am I doing the right thing? Am I good enough?), and fear (can I make it? What if I fail?)

Through it all my mantra was—I have to do what I would want my daughter to do.

What force made me surrender my choices and actions at the altar of love for my daughter? Where did these thoughts come from?

Life was too busy to pause and seek answers.

Until a fortuitous evening in October 2018 when, ironically while researching the life of a great Seer Patañjali I got my answer.

I was standing at the sanctum sanctorum by Lord Śiva's magnificent form at the Sri Nataraja temple at Chidambaram,

South India. Here, the legendary seer Patanjali's life is enshrined within the walls of the temple. As I stood in front of the Lord's magnificent bronze form aglow with the nearby oil lamps, Patanjali's yearning to see the Lord's dance and decision to walking thousands of miles on treacherous terrain to manifest his heartfelt desire flashed in my mind. I was trying to fathom the depth of his desire and devotion, the strength of his will, when another thought interjected: Was it desire that came from somewhere deep within me 12 years ago? Was the whisper I heard from somewhere deep within really a desire, that made me take steps to become the woman I wanted my daughter to be?

Excited at that prospect, I began a 'me-search.' I consciously attended to my desires and acted on them. What I found over time was this:

> when we attend to desires we can create harmony between what we truly want and what we actually do. There is no hypocrisy, self-doubt or confusion.

This sense of harmony bears upon how we live into our values. I experienced values in me I had till then only seen in others; courage to move forward in spite of fears, strength to act, the capacity for love, forgiveness and compassion. Where I once felt fragmented and unworthy of love, I now felt whole and worthy. Incidentally, it was at this time I met Sagar (now my husband) who reflected the same qualities.

Following my desire thus made my very ordinary life an enchanting one.

I am not implying that I live an incredibly joyful, "happily-ever-after" kind of life. However, if I were to measure life on a continuum of well-being and ask myself the questions: Am I happier, more compassionate, less frustrated, and more at peace now than I was five or ten years ago? The answer is a resounding yes! I am certainly happier on a day-to-day basis. Overall, I can say this for sure: understanding my desires has given power to my choices and significantly empowered my life.

It is with this conviction that I wish to unlock the power of desires to you by redrafting an ancient philosophical paradigm to tap into our highest destiny:

> You are your desires.
> As your Desires, so your Will,
> As your Will, so your Action,
> As your action, so your Destiny[2].

---

[2] Bṛhadāraṇyaka Upaniṣhad 4.4.5;
   kāmamaya evāyaṃ puruṣa iti; sa yathākāmobhavati tatkraturbhavati, yat kraturbhavati bhavati tatkarmakurute, yatkarma kurute tad abhisaṃpadyate

UNLOCKING THE POWER OF DESIRES

The wisdom template is underpinned by desire being the "seed"[3] of "immense potentiality", as the force of the manifest world itself. From this perspective, the human experience of desiring a certain kind of life then becomes the manifestation of the primal force, the great potential within each of us to shape our highest destiny. This is because desiring and acting on a desire bring forth qualities of the soul energy; love, enthusiasm, courage, daring, risk-taking, intelligence, fortitude, generosity and compassion. For the seers thus, spiritual ascension and engaging in world matters did not operate in isolation but in the seamless flow of our life's experiences.

At the core of this flow is the dynamic play between what we truly desire out of life and what we actually do about it. As simple as this may sound, in practice the truth of our contradictory nature, the need to impress more than express, digital addictions and seductions, and being "constantly caught up in reactivity" distract the free flow between the social and the spiritual aspects of our life. Hence, we need to mindfully create and manage the flow of desires between them in ways that are enjoyable,

---

[3] Rig Veda Book 10, Hymn:129.4: Thereafter rose Desire in the beginning. Desire, the primal seed and germ of Spirit.

engaging, enlightening (leading to deeper knowledge), and thereby beneficial, and transformational to us and others.

I will share just how to do that in this book. I will introduce you to the desire-template and its concomitant forces and define how each of its forces influences and impacts the social and spiritual aspects of your life so you can experience the joy that comes from attending to these forces in your life. To keep it simple (as much as that is even possible) and an accessible practice, I share my personal experiences and those of friends and family who generously shared their stories. I purposefully limited my data sample for two reasons: firstly to obviate our need to connect with media influencers and famous people for inspiration, when we are surrounded by people in our homes and backyards, who in their own ways are quietly leading remarkable lives. I tell their stories so you can imagine what is possible for you. Secondly, to understand desire intimately I needed to see it unfold in the lives of people I knew personally and deeply. These folks exemplify the most critical insight I have gained in my journey as a desire researcher. It forms the premise of this book: Desires empower each of us to shape our present and future, who we are and who we are meant to become.

I underpin the desire framework on an ancient wisdom template for a few reasons. First among them being, that's how I learned to articulate life experiences from my grandmother. I was greatly influenced by my late maternal grandmother Sitarama, for whom there was no grief, concern or issue that did not find resolve in our scriptures. It is because of her that I have deep faith that against all the loneliness, and chaos present-day living has thrown us into, we have in us the power of desires to overcome turbulence and have the life we want. Secondly, the wisdom of seers is eternal truths that are as rational as they are practical. As such they have withstood the test of time for over 3000 years and give us every reason to implicitly trust their teaching. Like a compass, their wisdom shines an illuminating light on the path of desires so we can navigate and orient our journey toward our highest destiny.

I offer this book to all of you inhabiting a range of emotional landscapes: those who are unsure of what they want out of life, those who question its meaning and their purpose in it, those who think they are not doing enough with their life and want to find meaningful outlets, those who doubt the power of their desires, those who want to feel empowered, those who, like me, are woefully lost in a web of multiple desires and seek clarity, those who feel a deep unsettling chasm exists between what they do outside and how they feel inside, and those who feel a nagging, a restlessness that 'something is off.'

So whether you are a homemaker, student, artist, scientist, etc., regardless of religious affiliation, caste distinction, and other cultural tropes, the wisdom of seers will guide you to unlock and tap the power of your desires so you can lead a more fulfilling life and own your destiny, rather than play its victim.

But first, let's talk about the one thing we are uncomfortable addressing—

Desires as a tainted source of inappropriate sexual behavior and material cravings.

THE ELEPHANT IN THE ROOM: LET'S TALK DESIRES

Desire, unfortunately, like much else around us has had its share of ups and downs. No other word in our scriptures has been held to more rigorous admonishing as desires. It has been misrepresented, misunderstood, condemned, and reductively paraded in the context of sexuality and materiality.

I have lost count of the number of times people have asked if I was writing about women's desire, or human sexuality or, as in one instance, The Kāma Sūtra. My response to that query was always received with a befuddled expression.

So let's move on to address the two frames of desires and clarify which frame holds the subject matter of this book.

By definition, desire is the primordial energy that rests within us as a deep wanting, an urge, calling us to manifest the qualities of our soul's energy. In everyday life, it is about making choices and taking actions driven by a deep desire to connect, engage and harmonize our personal attributes and aptitude with our duties and obligations in society.

When desire was held within this frame, it was celebrated. People had a strong moral compass and upheld values of community, inclusion, compassion, and harmony. In later years, this energy was anthropomorphized in the image of Goddess Shakti.

Centuries later, another frame resurfaced in a rapidly evolving, complex society. Greed, lust and an overall disintegration of values and morality became a way of life. It was at this time that social and religious leaders denounced desire as the single biggest obstacle on the path to our inherently spiritual nature. Over generations, this one-sided rhetoric seared into our collective consciousness. The journey to our highest destiny on the wings of desire was thus clipped.

Now, in the absence of any mandated directives from our institutions, I believe recourse to traditional wisdom is the way forward.

For starters, just look around you. The power of desire is everywhere.

Everything we know and understand in any field, be it in mathematics, astronomy, alchemy, arts, sciences, business, computers, etc. has its origin in desire:

> A desire to understand,
> A desire to know more,
> A desire to evolve, to transform, and ultimately,
> A desire to go beyond the horizon of knowledge.

Correspondingly, everything we want for ourselves has its essence in desires. We are simply hardwired to follow the path of desires for a variety of reasons:

To seek and find meaning.

To be like someone.

To evolve, to transform, and transcend to our inherent compassionate and blissful nature.

It is because of this hardwiring, "You are your Desires," and each of us is attracted to desires in our own way.

How to Use This Book

The intention of this book is to draw you toward the empowering energy of your desires as a 'living out' everyday experience. With that intention, I articulate my observation, understanding, and experience of desires in three parts. I look at them by turns, through different lenses: teaching of seers as recorded in Vedic texts, mythology, memoirs, and conversations with friends and family.

In part 2, (this being part 1)—**Ārṣa Dharma**, I bring to life the wisdom of seers and follow it by prescribed rules. I then focus on each of the variables on the path: age, personality and circumstance, what they mean, and how you can identify your heartfelt desires based on these variables.

Toward the end, I offer a "zoom-in" label. The zoom-in labels are intended to help you reflect on what you have just read and put down in writing, your experiences. This tool has helped me to objectively look at my life experiences without giving in to the temptation of being critical or judgmental toward myself and trying to 'diagnose' a problem.

In Part 3, Yoga Mārgam, I build on the ideas in part 2 and underscore the wisdom teachings of each of the four forces: desire, Will, action and destiny with real-life narratives.

I want to make it clear that each of the forces is a vast topic in itself. It can be viewed through a religious or philosophical lens and interpreted in different ways. My interest and focus are on how to assimilate the wisdom of our seers into our lives in today's world, as an everyday, actionable practice. With this intention, I offer a bird's view of what is to be expected:

Desire: I look at three kinds of desires that we experience every day—egocentric, obsessive egocentric, and heartfelt and I explore how to identify heartfelt desires.

Will: I present Will as a sacred contract between our faith in our ability and devotion to our tasks and I explore how to strengthen our Will. It is my intention to capitalize the W, when talking of Will as a force of desire, to distinguish it from the 'will' we use to express a future tense.

Action: I look at three kinds of actions (corresponding to the three desires): everyday obligations, prohibited actions, and selfless actions and I explore how to manifest desires through ethical and moral actions.

Destiny: I distinguish between destiny and the highest destiny and I tell the story of my maternal uncle Dr. Parameshwara Rao.

At the end of each component, the zoom-in session provides tools to identify your desires, cultivate steadfast will, and map your actions. At the end of part 3, I give you a vision board that will give you an overview of the activities that drive your curiosity and interest, and that you enjoy, so you can lead a life you truly desire.

In the last part, **Moving forward and up**, I summarize the DWAD template in a model called R.I.S.E, the Relational, Intellectual, Spiritual, and Emotional outcomes of integrating your outer and inner personality. I also present some of the obstacles in the journey toward our highest destiny.

A suggestion:

The zoom-in exercises are meant for you to observe, reflect and experiment. I made them based upon my experiences with workbooks created by luminaries in the field of happiness (Tal-ben Shahar)[4], wholehearted living (Brene Brown)[5] Peace and meaning (Eknath Easwaran),[6] joy and activism (Karen Walrond)[7], and self-compassion (Kristin Neff and Christopher Germer)[8] and my professional experience of teaching for 38 years. I want you to know that I am not a therapist or a psychologist of any kind. I am a me-searcher, always observing and intrigued by those who have embraced their lives fully and lived wholeheartedly. In the same vein,

---

[4] Tal Ben Shahar, Happier, 2007

[5] https://brenebrown.com/wholeheartedinventory/

[6] Eknath Easwaran, Take your time. How to find Patience, Peace and Meaning. 2006

[7] Karen Walrond, The Lightmaker's Manifesto: How to work for change without losing your joy,2021

[8] Kristin Neff and Christopher Germer, The mindful Self-Compassion workbook: A proven way to accept yourself, build inner strength and thrive, 2018

I am no exponent of Vedic philosophy; I am a practitioner of one of its templates on desire.

As you go along with the zoom-in exercises, take as much time as you need and make sure you are comfortable answering the questions, if not, set them aside until you are ready. Consider them suggestions and an opportunity to pause, reflect deeply, and put down practical notes and actionable ideas.

Feel free to change your answers or not answer them if it causes you some discomfort or if you need more time. I understand most of us are too hard on ourselves. We sabotage ourselves with our constant self-doubt regarding our abilities, capabilities, and strengths. I request that you give yourself honest feedback either by writing or voice recording—whatever floats your boat. The integrity with which you answer the questions is the key to unlocking your highest destiny.

As you prepare to venture along the path and the journey of desires, I give you the mythological story of Ganga's descent to the earth as an archetype of how desire will unfold within you.

GANGA, AN ARCHETYPE OF DESIRE

It was a tradition in ancient India for a newly coronated king to pay his respects to his ancestors. And so, when Bhagiratha, was crowned king of the Ikshvaku dynasty, his Guru Trithala took him to the enshrined monument of his ancestors. Here, for the first time, the king heard of the sins committed by his great uncles and the consequent curse that they could not attain salvation after death. The only way to release them from the curse, the Guru explained was for the king to undergo intense meditation for years and beseech the mighty Ganges River, personified as Ganga, to flow on their ashes. Only the purity of her waters would absolve the king's forefathers of their sins.

Hearing this, Bhagiratha handed over the administration of the kingdom to his ministers and retired into the forest to undertake deep penance.

It is known that the Ganga, the most sacred of rivers heeds the call of a chosen few. She endlessly tests their faith, devotion, and perseverance. So it was that, decades went by before Ganga appeared before the king and promised to fulfill his desire.

But, she warned him, the power of her cascading flow would shatter and destroy the earth. Therefore, it was incumbent on the king to protect the earth and his people from the destructive power of her cascading flow. Accordingly, the king appealed to Lord Śiva to contain her flow.

At the predetermined time, as promised she cascaded down to earth. As she fell toward the earth Lord Śiva contained her force within the locks of his hair, from where she flowed in different directions as tributaries. The Ganges today is also called Bhagirathi in honor of this great king Bhagiratha.

Like the Ganges, we will experience desire like its powerful flow, breaking through barriers and glass ceilings. At such a time we will need to harness the power of our desire through ethical and moral actions. When desire is thus channelized, it brings forth the power of Will (Icchā Shakti) to guide our actions (Kriyā Shakti) and gives us the wisdom (Jnāna Shakti) to know how and where to land that action, until it leads us to the ocean of our destiny.

On the other hand, it can also be, as happens to many of us, that many little desires meander along like tributaries, with varying potency of will and action, until circumstances cause a dramatic confluence toward our highest destiny.

I hope the stories presented in the pages of this book will resonate with you and inspire you to live fully from the heart. I can't think of a more important time than right now. I share snippets of my life along the way and those of friends and family members whom I have known deeply, in the hope that you will seek and write your own version of "I am my desire."

There is no doubt the exercises will call for your courage. Holding a mirror to your life is not easy, let alone baring your heart. Jump into it fearlessly, wholeheartedly.

Where you are right now is a great place to start.

Before you move on, take a pause and think about this interpretation of a quote from 'A course in Miracles' by Marianne Williamson. [9] I hope it resonates with you as it did with me:

> Our deepest fear is not that we are inadequate.
> Our deepest fear is that we are powerful beyond measure.
> It is our light, not our darkness that most frightens us.
> We ask ourselves, who am I to be brilliant, gorgeous, talented and fabulous?
> ……Your playing small does not serve the world.
> There's nothing enlightened about shrinking so that other people won't feel insecure around you.
> We were born to make manifest the glory of
> God that is within us.
> It's not just in some of us; it's in everyone.
> And as we let our own light shine,
> we unconsciously give other people
> permission to do the same.
> As we are liberated from our own fear,
> Our presence automatically liberates others.

---

[9] Marianne Williamson. A return to love. Loc 190 of 301. Kindle

. . . .

PART 2

ĀRṢA DHARMA,
THE WISDOM OF SEERS

I am desire itself, if that desire is in harmony with the purpose of life.

The Bhagavad Gita 7.11

INTRODUCTION

The term Ārṣa (derived from the Sanskrit root 'rsh,') refers to the tradition of seers in ancient India and the term Dharma (derived from the root 'dhri') means upholding prescribed principles for the well-being of society and spiritual experience of bliss by its people.[10]

Since Dharma applies to everyone from all walks of life, its concept has varied applications across the spectrum of social roles and behavior. The Dharma of a political administrator will be very different from the Dharma of an artist or that of a homemaker. The ultimate goal of Dharma, however, remains common to all: the spiritual experience of bliss.

Therefore, it is necessary to contour the application of Dharma in its specific context to avoid misrepresentation. In the context of this book, I present Dharma as the principles that must be practiced in thought, word, and deed if we choose to follow the path of heartfelt desires and shape our highest destiny.

---

[10] Vaiśheṣhika Sūtra 1.1.2 defines Dharma as "yato'bhyudayaniḥśreyasasiddhiḥ sa dharmaḥ." Meaning, Dharma is the path towards the spiritual experience of bliss. Taken from Swami Mukyananda: Hinduism, The eternal Dharma. An evolutionary and Historical perspective.

LIVING BY THE WISDOM OF SEERS

It is the spring of 2017. The 500-hour, Yoga Teacher Training program is in session at the Himalayan Institute, Poconos, Pennsylvania. In the sunlit assembly hall, 54 enthusiastic learners are preparing to settle into adhomukha svanasana (downward dog).

On the floor I am paddling my feet, shifting my pelvis, exploring the best way to experience the asana in my body. As I settle into the pose, I feel my teacher Shari's hands on my shoulder. This would be the first time that I sense the energy of a gentle touch in my practice. From somewhere deep within the muscles of my shoulder, I feel a loosening, a letting go, an opening of space. I take a deep breath and as I exhale my shoulders expand, my chest sinks lower, my pelvis lifts, my spine lengthens, my hands stabilize and I feel…Peace. I close my eyes to savor the moment.

This is Shari's class, a place where the practice of self-love and compassion begins on the mat and every breath becomes an opportunity to look deep within. She holds the space for us to acknowledge and let go of emotional wounds and seek kindness from within.

From the first time I met Shari I was taken by her lithesome regal demeanor, her compassionate face framed by short honey-blonde hair, and the knowing in her eyes. In class, her cues are both kind and witty. By opening a path of kindness in Yoga practice she leads us on an inward journey, guiding us with the wisdom of Yoga sūtras to become deeply aware of emotions and arising thoughts. By the end of our training, each of us in our own way learns to trust the power we behold and our heart's innate intelligence to lead us on a path of self-empowerment and, self -acceptance.

In the four years since my training, I continue to hear Shari's voice guiding my practice. Unsurprisingly, my teaching of dance and Yoga hinges on what I learned from her about love and kindness. I am but one of the hundreds of practitioners whose personal and professional life has been profoundly impacted and influenced by Shari's teaching. All because 50 years ago, she followed her heart to seek a connection, an anchor, a meaning to life.

Shari grew up in a middle-class American Catholic household in Los Angeles. Her parents were not the kind that demonstrated their love openly either toward each other or their seven children. It was not a particularly unhappy childhood, neither was it a happy, memorable one. By the time Shari was 13 years old, she felt a yearning for love, kindness and meaning in life.

In her 20's she came into the practice of Yoga. Something in its practice and philosophy stirred emotions 'deep within'. She was particularly struck by how kind, gentle and soothing it was.

Soon she wanted to know more, to explore in-depth. She had mastered the technique of asanas as far as she wanted to get with it. She now wanted to get to the core of Yoga philosophy and embody the principles in practice. It resonated deeply with her. She said, "The more I studied Yoga, the more my heart was filled with gratitude that a seer put it together. It made me feel: **I can be more of who I want to be.**"

All through this time she was working during the day, studying in the evenings and teaching Yoga at a nearby community college. She was always living in debt. But she remained unfazed by her dire financial situation. She recalls believing, "If I follow my heart, my longing to study Yoga, and a longing to teach, everything else will fall into place." Of her many teachers she says: "When I was ready, the teacher that I needed at that time came to me, literally."

One day in 2001, while traveling with her Guru, Amma Karunamayi in Sedona (Arizona), she looked around at the people who had come to bid farewell and felt for the very first time an overwhelming abundance of love; for her life, for her husband Mark and for her teacher.

The love she felt carried her through challenging times when she and Mark became caregivers to her parents, who were both simultaneously diagnosed with dementia. When I asked her what prompted the difficult decision to live with and care for parents who never showed her any affection, she replied:

" They don't know what love is and if they die without knowing love in their life, that is what they will bring into their next life. I couldn't allow that to happen. I wanted them to have an experience of being cared for and loved."

In 2008, when her mother passed away 10 days after her dad, she recalled:

"I was sitting in the room with Mark and my mom. When she passed away we felt as though the whole room was illumined by bliss. We sat there for an hour in silence in the field of grace and felt we had done the most important work of our lives."

As we came toward the end of our interview Shari said, "All I want now is to go deep within myself and know and experience everything there is to the self."

In her desire to seek love, and kindness,

In her unshakable resolve to find a practice that was loving and kind,

In the long years of exploration and practice of Yoga,

In transforming her life through the teachings of Yoga,

In acknowledging love and abundance within herself and for those around her,

In serving her parents with unconditional love and devotion,

In experiencing a state of mind 'illumined by bliss' in the 'field of grace,'

Shari experienced the highest and noblest energy of her soul. This is the highest destiny seers talk about. In such moments, we experience a desire-less state of self-transcendence; our hearts know only love and our minds, peace.

Shari's life thus exemplified the socio-spiritual template of seers:

> You are your deep driving **Desire**,
> As your desire, so your **Will,**
> As your will, so your **Action,**
> As your action, so your **Destiny.**

I refer to this as the DWAD path and place its four components as the coordinates to our soul energy.

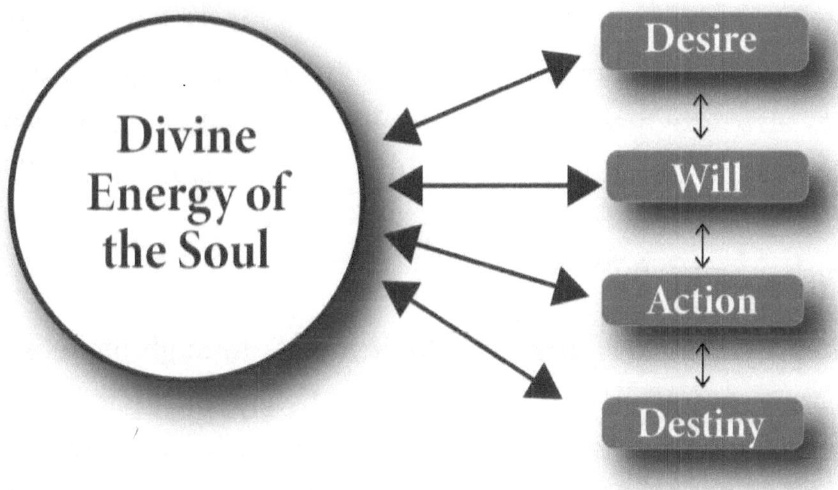

Fig 1. Coordinates to our soul energy

THE DWAD TEMPLATE UNDER THE ARC OF DHARMA

When seers of ancient India left behind a spiritual legacy they recognized the importance of self -fulfillment (Sva-Dharma) for the prosperity of a nation. Simply put, a frustrated individual is not going to contribute to the well-being of his community but a person who is personally fulfilled will reach out to help others. They also recognized, that we have the propensity to carry many things to an extreme and self-fulfillment can lead to unbridled selfishness and hubris. So they laid down the principles within which we must fulfill our desires.

When we thus look at the DWAD template through the lens of Dharma, not all desires will lead to our highest destiny. Only certain desires that we manifest with a strong Will and appropriate actions will help us harmoniously integrate the spiritual and social aspects of our lives. Seers called the spiritual and social aspects of life, **Nivritti Dharma — The process of 'going inward' and Pravritti Dharma—the process of "moving forward".**[11] The two aspects are, as you will read below, interwoven into our personality.

Now to integrate the two aspects of life you must:

[11] Swamy Mukhyananda: Hinduism, The Eternal Dharma: An evolutionary and Historical perspective, p.63

Identify your unique heartfelt **desires,** cultivate a strong **will** and follow it up with appropriate actions

As you endeavor on this path, your experiences will be unique and differ widely from those of others. The three key variables that drive how you experience and bring desire to life are: **age, personality, and circumstance**[12]. Within the orbit of these variables, desire must be in concordance with one's age, aligned to one's unique personality, and hold meaning within a given circumstance.

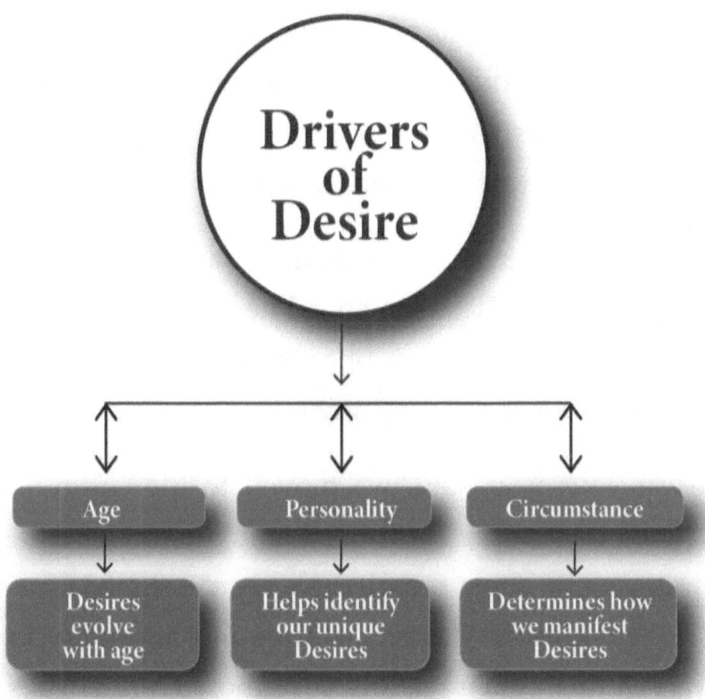

Fig.2 Drivers of desire

I offer my mother's life to show you how these three variables serve our well-being:

....

[12] Ibid. p.84

My mother Aruna (henceforth addressed as ma) grew up in a traditional, patriarchal South Indian family. She was raised by a somewhat conservative father and a progressive mother. My grandmother played the veena (a string instrument) and her melodies set the stage for my mother's love for singing as a young four-year-old.

When ma was a teenager she yearned to learn music. However, the circumstance of living in a village meant there were no opportunities for any formal training. So she taught herself to sing by listening to movie songs over the radio. She sang in two languages, Telugu, her native tongue, and Hindi. Since she did not speak or understand Hindi, she decided to learn the language. She found the nearest Hindi teacher a few miles away. With her brother's help, she walked to the classes during the weekend.

Once married, ma began her new life in the largely Hindi-speaking megapolis, Mumbai. There she honed her skills in spoken Hindi. Life as a homemaker was busy. She kept up her love for music by singing to the three of us every night.

When I was four years old, we moved to the cultural hub of India, Chennai. Here she auditioned and got accepted to sing in the All-India-Radio choir. Simultaneously she signed up to enroll in Bachelor's and later Master's courses in Philosophy in Hindi literature. All this, while making sure there were always warm food and a welcoming smile when we got home from school every day.

When the choir disbanded, she worked on and released a few independent music albums in five different languages.

At 57, an opportunity came her way to write dialogs for a movie being dubbed from one language (Marathi) to another (Telugu). She had no experience. But she jumped into it anyway. A few years later her brother asked her if she could complete his project on translating a book on Swami Rama from English to Telugu. My mother readily agreed and this opened a whole new world of creative projects.

Today at 77, she continues to translate a wide range of books from English to Telugu. She works with a fierce determination whether at home in India or with us in the United States. She writes for anywhere between five to six hours a day. In between, she cooks for us (when she is visiting), goes for walks, watches movies, and makes the time to do all the little things that add value and meaning to her life.

It is by no measure an easy achievement. She dared to pursue her desires throughout her life. rather than suppress them. She fearlessly dove into every opportunity that came her way, rather than weave a narrative along the lines of 'I cannot do it because...' And she did so under varying circumstances—before and after having kids, traveling to different places—and in spite of prevailing reductionist cultural norms that a woman must be a domestic goddess first and foremost and only then, if allowed, indulge in her interests. For her, there was no conflicting or competing expectation between who she truly was (artiste/writer/mom/wife) and what she put out in the world (music/author/mom/wife).

When I asked her how she did it all in a quiet sort of way, her matter-of-fact reply was "I just couldn't imagine one without the other, I had to sing, I had to write and I had to take care of my family," and with a shrug, she added, "It is just who I am."

Graphically Shari's and Ma's process looks like this:

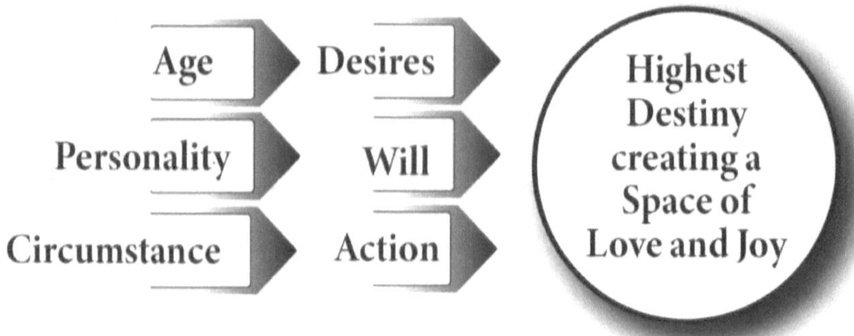

Fig. 3. Key Drivers of DWAD

Now let's unpack the four drivers of desire individually and zoom-in to see how desires evolve with age, what your personality profile is and how your particular circumstance determines how you bring forth desires.

1) Age

Every age points to new desires and a new level of paying attention to them. What we want at age 15 will be very different from what we want, say a decade later. Every few years we orient ourselves to desires differently.

This is why attending to our desires is so interesting. Some desires continue to hold our interest and curiosity for much of our lives, while others morph into something else. As we grow and transform, so do our desires.

For this reason, in ancient India a person's life-span was divided into four successive stages relating to their psychological and physical evolution, each corresponding to certain desires. Consider them to be a sequential flow rather than claustrophobic, boxed-in, stereotypical directives.

Student stage: This stage corresponds with the desire to understand life around us, and imbibe the values and principles that bind humanity.

House-holder stage: Here physical and material desires are fulfilled. We take care of others, experience appropriate sexual gratification, buy a house, save money and fulfill social/financial duties and responsibilities

Retirement stage: In the third stage of life, we retire from active paid service. We practice meditation, and mindfulness, volunteer, take courses that we long yearned for and give counsel to those who request it without seeking personal gain (Nishkāma karma). This prepares us for the last stage of our life.

Renunciation stage: We let go of our attachments, and our ego and meditate upon creating a space of peace, love and bliss within us.

2) Personality

There are two aspects to our personality: Core spiritual self and social self. These correspond with the 'going inward' and 'moving forward' process.

Our Core self comprises our authentic personality; who we truly are. It includes the principles or virtues we actually live by (not the ones we profess), emotions, and intellectual capacity (ability to think, learn, assimilate new experiences, and discern right from wrong)[13].

Our social self comprises (I group them into two): i) skill and aptitude, and, ii) behavior and actions.

When I look back on my life, I can tie down all my missteps and frustrations—starting a business (no head for it), working in an office (can't sit behind a desk), wanting to be a YouTube influencer (not a social media-type), to barking up the wrong tree of desires. All these were completely misaligned to my core self (what I truly wanted) and social self (what I projected).

Ma on the other hand lined up her creative interests with her personality. Did she ever doubt her skill in music or writing? Her cryptic response, "Where is the time to think of all that?" She simply lived from her heart, not giving pause to self-doubts and influencers. Similarly, Shari too felt deeply compelled to find a practice that would fulfill her. When desires run deep they align with our personality and we find ways to manifest them against all odds.

Let's take a closer look at each of these variables:

i) Virtues

Values are what we truly believe in, what we hold as important.

Seers declared that we practice and live by our virtues in how we act (karmaṇā), think (manasā), and in the way we speak

---

[13] I include only those relevant to his study. Faith, belief and physical capacity are implied.

(vāchā). They laid down the values we must observe every day. I list some of the fundamental values across Vedic texts and their derivatives[14].

Joyful	Truth	Non-stealing(integrity)	Fearlessness/courage
Fortitude	Forgiveness	Patience	Adventurous/risk-taking spirit
Humility	Love/compassion	Empathy	Faith
Respectful	Responsible	Dutiful	Gentleness
Accountability	Reliability	Creative	Commitment
Collaboration	Steadfast	Community	Perseverance
Freedom	Peaceful	Knowledge	Inclusive
Self-control	Generosity	Absence of betrayal	Wisdom
Learning	Curiosity	Optimism	Non-violence
Efficiency	Control of senses	Restraint from finding fault in us and others	Honesty/straightforwardness

ii) Emotions

Our emotions are powerful indicators of desires that serve our well-being.

We all have an emotional threshold, a point at which we are happy, sad, frustrated or angry. I have a low threshold for anger. Which means I get irritated or angry quickly. But, when I am teaching or am immersed in research activity, the intrinsically gratifying experience propels me toward positive emotions of well-being and joy.

---

[14] These are often mentioned values, others being manifestations or derivatives of the same.

It is for this reason, that when we are on the rightful path to our heartfelt desire we subconsciously cultivate **emotional resilience**—instead of copping out the easy way, we 'hang in', address our emotions and navigate through them during rough times. This is a particularly big take-away in cultures where emotions are commonly suppressed for fear of social ridicule and shame.

iii) Intellectual Capacity

Intellectual capacity refers to our ability to discern right from wrong, be curious, be open to new experiences and new ways of learning and also determine how much we can do i.e., how wide and deep we can go to express our desires.

For example, I never thought of myself as a writer. But when I decided to share my experiences and my findings, writing became an exciting prospect since I have always enjoyed reading. I took up the task of reading different genres seriously—highlighting interesting sentence formation, expression, voice, etc.—I went wide.

Then I went deep.

While writing this book, some days ideas flowed and my writing was uninterrupted for an hour. At other times for 30 minutes. Within this time frame, I would write in multiple sessions throughout the day. That is my intellectual capacity. During these periods of time, I was oblivious to the construction work in the neighborhood or my neighbor's dog barking at every passerby.

Now to the **social self:**

i) Skill and Aptitude

Our skill is the ability we have to do something. It can be anything: educational or work-related, organizing the house, organizing a party, taking photographs, etc. Aptitude is our inherent disposition to do something. It comes easily to us.

In recent years, psychologists[15] identified three approaches to work: job, career, and calling.

A job is what we do to simply pay the bills. There is no expectation or higher purpose beyond the pay check. A career is what we build as we go up the corporate ladder with an expectation for higher income and motivated by the power and prestige it accords. A calling is what we must do because it gives us meaning and helps us connect and engage with others in a deeply fulfilling way.

Our skill set and aptitude can be aligned with a career or a job, but it is as a calling that we integrate our spiritual and social nature and embrace our authentic selves. Heartfelt desires are a calling.

The Bhagavad Gita says, we all come into this world to perform certain tasks that are aligned with our personalities. In doing such work, whether it is perceived as low-mid-high level, a job, or a career, we will personally take more responsibilities, contribute more, learn, and expand our skills and capabilities. Such work enhances our overall well-being because it is "in accordance

---

[15] Amy Wrzesniewski and Jane E. Dutton. https://positiveorgs.bus.umich.edu/wp-content/uploads/Crafting-a-Job_Revisioning-Employees.pdf

with the same cosmic forces that hold the world together—unity, truth, love—and all our actions are imbued with their power."[16]

ii) Behavior and Actions

Our behavior and actions are a manifestation of the principles and virtues we actually live by.

I came into my heartfelt desire not so much by thinking about what I wanted to do, but by observing what I was actually doing and how, as a result, I was behaving with others.

Here are some teachings on the right behavior and action as espoused in Vedic texts. These are given as instructions to a student who after completing formal education is stepping out into the world. I co-opted and presented them in the first person as they show up in our everyday lives. These are not exhaustive. Feel free to add to the list as they apply to your life.

My actions reflect one or more of the following behaviors:

> I am respectful to everyone: I listen and I am thoughtful toward others
> I speak the truth: I don't lie and cheat on myself or others
> I am generous with my time and share my knowledge/ information.
> I am careful not to cause harm to others or myself by word, thought or deed
> I practice integrity in all that I do

16 Bhagavad Gita. Eknath Easwaran p. 414

I articulate my feelings rather than expect others to decipher them

I have faith in my ability to complete a chosen task

I choose what is right and I check into my values (Dharma) when I have to take a tough decision or when I am in doubt

I take responsibility for my actions. I don't blame others or play the "victim" card

I seek counsel when I don't know something. I am not too proud to ask

I am accountable for my well-being. I don't blame fate and destiny for my choices and actions

I am open to new experiences, and new ways of thinking

iii) Circumstance

Circumstance is the social and cultural context within which we seek to fulfill our desires. Our social and cultural environment—family ideals, cultural norms, and financial situation—determines how we engage with ourselves and others in our different relationships and experience of desires.

There are so many different circumstances under which we come into our desires; time, available resources (funding and financial commitments), family support, and encouragement.

For example, for any aspiring student of Yoga or Indian performing arts, India is the place to be in. Excellent teachers provide guidance in various meditative techniques and art immersions in verdant surroundings. It provides students the opportunity to be part of a collective whose desires reflect their own, with whom they share, learn, and grow. Seers called such a collective Sahṛdaya (one with whom we share a heartfelt connection). But how many can afford the travel and other logistics? Can they take time off? Will their family support their decision? So many concerns have to be addressed to take our desires to the next level.

It was at such a crossroads that Shari took up a job that came her way, and worked hard at it so she could pay for her trips to India. While in India, she was willing to adapt to the prevailing cultural norms, serve her teacher, and do whatever else was required of her at the ashram. In her desire to learn Yoga from a particular teacher in India, Shari inadvertently integrated her social and spiritual aspirations.

Zoom-in

Profiling You

An exercise on knowing who you are is a spiritual practice of mindfulness. The following is a preliminary step. Take your time in doing these exercises. They will require you to :

Ruminate on your desires

Look back on your life and think of the many desires you had growing up. List them by the ones you enjoyed for a short while, the ones you gave up, and those that continue to hold your interest.

Reflect on how you felt at these times.

Name Your Values

List two or three values you identify as your core values. If you are not sure what they are, or to double-check on the values you listed, here is an exercise.

Think of three or four people you admire. Write their names down. Against each of them write down every single attribute you admire in each of them. They can be living or dead, or fictional. The common traits that pop up when you describe them, are your core values.

Another way of identifying your core values is by paying attention to your attributes. This is how I identified my core values:

Courage: For me, courage is asking tough questions in personal relationships and giving honest feedback.

Family: I demonstrate this by preparing meals and spending quality time with them every day and just being available whenever needed—it can be going for walks, chatting, watching movies, or taking care of my grandchildren.

As you put down your own values, highlight them. You may not realize it yet, but your values are valuable tools in identifying your heartfelt desires.

Feel your emotions

Our native emotion is love and we value truth and unity. This is the benchmark of spiritual living.

Dig deep into your emotions, the why and how of it: List how you feel about everything you do and note the activities you enjoy and those you don't.

In her book 'Atlas of the Heart' Brené Brown lists 87 emotions and experiences. You may download the list at https://brenebrown.com/resources/atlas-of-the-heart-list-of-emotions to help you identify your feelings.

Attend to your skills and intellectual capacity: List all the skills that come to you naturally and those you desire to acquire. It can be anything like organizing, managing, creating, building, exploring, or cooking. A way to identify them is to check-in to see if they are enjoyable, engaging, and enlightening (deepen your knowledge)—what I call the three E's.

What do you enjoy doing? What are you curious about? How wide and deep are you willing to go to hone your skill?

Note: There is no such thing as an unimportant feeling, irrelevant trait, or useless skill. Everything that shapes who you are, is worthy of attention. Just so you know, one of my skills is to write from the right to the left side of a page, with mirror-image letters. It has no measurable worth in any currency (so far). Nonetheless, I put it down as a skill. If you can or want to do something, go ahead and list it.

Check-in on your Behaviors and Actions

What behavior do your actions reflect? Feel free to pick from the list of behaviors presented above or add as needed.

Your Circumstance

Look back on your life and note how your circumstances shaped your choice in education, activities or training in specific skills.

What activities did you consistently pursue?

How did your circumstances affect your choice?

The above exercises are meant to raise a mirror to your life and help you gage the congruence between your inner desires at different times in your life, (under varying circumstances) and how you lived your life thus far.

The practices above will reveal much about how your core self and social self-evolved over a period of time, the values you behold and the behaviors that best define you. Moving forward we will look at how you can leverage your desires as a prelude to the choices you will make, so you can shape the life you truly want.

To show you what it means to manifest your desires and live wholeheartedly, I leave you with a definition of wholehearted living by Brené Brown[17]:

> Wholehearted living is about engaging in our lives from a place of worthiness. It means cultivating the courage, compassion, and connection to wake up in the morning and think, No matter what gets done and how much is left undone, I am enough. It's going to bed at night thinking, Yes, I am imperfect and vulnerable and sometimes afraid, but that doesn't change the truth that I am also brave and worthy of love and belonging.

[17] Brené Brown. Gifts of Imperfection. Pg. 3, 2010

PART 3

YOGA MĀRGAM: ORIENTING OUR LIVES TO THE WISDOM OF SEERS

Subtler than the subtle, greater than the great,
In the heart of each living being, the Soul reposes.
One must earnestly desire to know that.

Katha Upanishad 1.2.20.
Chāndogyopaniṣad 8.1.1

INTRODUCTION

In the context of this book, I refer to Yoga Mārgam as a path we choose to mindfully assimilate desire, Will, and action, into our core (spiritual) self and outer (social) self to shape our highest destiny. Think of it as a "yoking" of the mind and heart, what we intellectually understand with what we intuitively know works best for us.

In this part, my intention is to bring your awareness into the 'anatomy' of each of the forces—desire, Will, action and destiny to help you articulate desires and shape your highest destiny.

To help you along, I offer three meditative practices that underlie our journey[18]:

1. Listening/hearing (Śravaṇa): This requires you to listen to others, gain their insights, understand particular choices and situations from different perspectives and ask the question, "What do I truly want"?

---

[18] Brihadaranyaka 4.5.6 : The Self, should be realized—should be heard of, reflected on and meditated upon.

ātmā vā are draṣṭavyaḥ śrotavyo mantavyo nidhidhyāsitavyo maitreyyātmani khalvare dṛṣṭe śrute mate vijñāta idaṃ sarvaṃ viditam ǀǀ

2. Contemplation (Manana): The next step is to weigh in on all your 'wants' and ask yourself: Why do I want to fulfill these desires? What is beneath the desire to lose weight? To learn music? Is the desire to "fix" a perceived problem or shortcoming in you? Is it to have more of what you already have? Is it something that will add meaning to your life?

3. Absorption (Nididhyāsana): The third stage brings together the first two practices. It involves framing your intention by articulating what you truly want and taking appropriate action.

The three practices do not flow in any order and are meant to help you look deeper within yourself before or during any activity you choose to undertake, be it starting a new project or trying to figure out what you want out of life. Whatever it may be, ultimately, the power in 'You are your desire' lies in what desires you tap into. The three practices along with the wisdom of seers will help bring your awareness to who you truly are, your authentic personality (core spiritual self and outer social self) and choose accordingly, so you can move forward and up.

DESIRE

. . . .

**To have a prayer, or a desire is a call of the heart,
A summons to fulfill our highest destiny.**

A Call of the Heart

One of my closest friends Madhuri (an alias) is a graphic designer by profession. As a young adult, inspired by her mother, an artist, she started to paint. Something about painting moved her deeply. In college, she decided to widen her artistic abilities and enrolled to study design. In the years it took to establish and build her business as a graphic designer, her love for painting was placed on the back-burner. Whenever she felt the urge to paint she fed herself with a narrative along the lines of "Why bother with something I am not good at?" or, "I have no time to paint."

Thus for more than 25 years, she silenced her inner craving. Every time the nagging feeling that something was missing in her life surfaced, she pushed it down, sweeping it under a large pile of 'to-do-in-the-future list'. She would look at the neat array of brushes, and the stacks of canvas in the cupboard with a wistful yearning.

As a result, my friend who is by nature sensitive and even-tempered, began off-loading her frustration and irritation on those she loved the most. Every time she unintentionally hurt someone she felt guilty and ashamed of her behavior. This became a pattern, the unintended consequence of suppressing deeply-felt desires.

Then in 2020 when the pandemic shut down the country she found herself with a lot of time on her hands and empty office space around her. Out of having nothing else to do, she picked up a brush and started to paint, first with some hesitancy, and then with growing confidence. Gradually she started to share her paintings with me. It started with one. With that, she was extremely self-critical about color, light, technique, etc. Then came another, then another. The more she did, the less critical she became. Very soon she was excited about other possibilities. It seemed like out of nowhere there was a sudden eruption of emotions. She painted an entire series on wild animals. I looked at them and was astounded! When the Black Lives Matter revolution in the United States reverberated across the globe, she painted a series of beautiful African tribal women. Through her painting, she began to express her true feelings.

There was a gradual unfolding of great joy and beauty within her. She was excited about life, of things that inspired her, and the ideas that filled her mind. She began to explore the innumerable ways those ideas could take shape and form on the canvas. She felt connected to her core self and this was reflected in how she socially engaged with family, friends, and everyday exigencies.

During this time, no doubt, the uncertainty of work and looming financial hardships were major concerns. But the moments of transcendence and joy that her art evoked overshadowed anxiety over her finances.

The central force behind such moments of joy, as well as frustration and irritation in all our lives, is—desire. To know what desires are aligned with our personality and give us joy, we have to understand the forces at play within us.

Three Forces of Desire

Desires flow within all of us. They are generally categorized as selfless desires and selfish desires. While talking to friends and relatives I observed a range of desires: desire for a close-knit family, beautiful house, good food, memorable experiences with friends, soulful music, etc., selfish desires for more and more of everything and, desires which come from deep within and give us an "optimal experience" (joy and transcendence) of our authentic personality.

I categorize them as:

Egocentric desires: These are "micro" desires such as love for color, travel, etc. They help you connect, share and engage with others, enjoy and explore the world, and lead you to your heartfelt desire.

Obsessive egocentric desires: These are obsessively selfish desires that go against social and spiritual values, and take you away from who you truly are.

Heartfelt desires: These integrate our egocentric desires in a way that is immersive as well as challenging, and facilitates meaningful connection with others. These reflect who you truly are.

Now, let's look at each of these desires in detail. I give quotidian examples of each desire based on my experience and observation of them.

Egocentric Desires

Like most South Indians, I love my morning cup of espresso coffee, every precious sip of it. For me, it has to be made in a particular way with the right proportions of milk, coffee, and sugar. I love the percolating sound, its nutty, smoky aroma, its creaminess ...every sense-tingling bit. The subtleties encourage a Zen-like concentration and attention to the present moment. After I make the coffee, I sit in a quiet corner to savor its flavors undisturbed (to my family's amusement). I relate to the 17th-century Japanese tea master Sen Stan who once said, "The taste of tea and the taste of Zen are the same.[19]"

This simple, pleasurable indulgence evokes a memory from 10,000 miles away, when in my twenties I woke up to the aromatic smell of freshly brewed coffee at home and enjoyed a cup with my dad. That was the only time in the day that we both would sit and chat. To this day coffee gives me an emotional context and adds meaning to my life.

Now, by indulging in this desire I am not hurting or causing inconvenience to anybody. Generally, these kinds of simple quotidian pleasures abound in all of us. For some it is food, for others, it is shopping, organizing their space, or playing

[19] Michael Pollan. This is your mind on Plants. P.125

video games. Overall, they create an emotional context, and to some degree positively contribute to our well-being. These are egocentric desires operating under the arc of Dharma.

We don't have to suppress these desires, we enjoy them. These desires while giving us a sensual experience of the world around us, also, as the name suggests, serve the ego. We can easily be misled into identifying who we are by the things we possess, achieve and accomplish. We can also get carried away by what others are doing and by trying to emulate them. **It is only when we rein in temptations and diversions of egocentric desire under the arc of Dharma, that our actions throw light on who we are, our thoughts, what we like and don't, how we feel, etc., and facilitate our journey into heartfelt desires.**

Here are a few such simple pleasures:

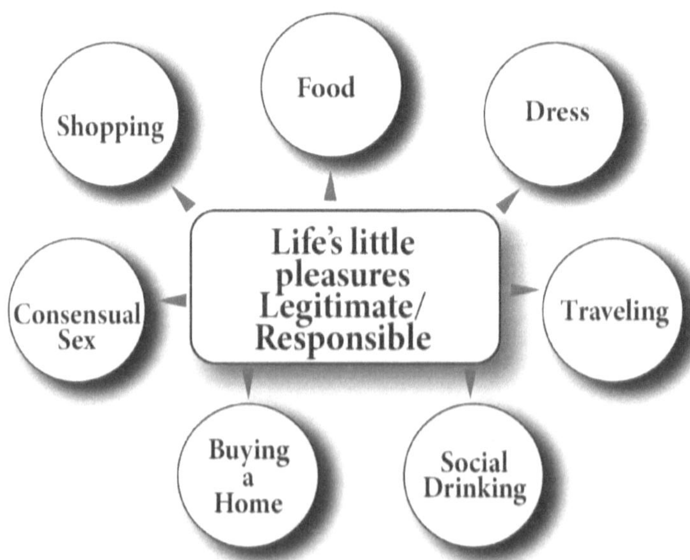

Fig.4. Everyday pleasures of egocentric desires.

In all of the above examples the pathway of egocentric desires is the senses (taste, smell, visual appeal, etc.). They give us an emotional context (invoke memories of shared activity with family and friends) and add meaning to our lives.

The parameters of egocentric desires under the arc of Dharma are:

1. They give us an enriching experience of the world around us. They help us connect, share, and engage with others.

2. They hold a mirror to our personality: what we like and don't, our beliefs, our attitude, our capacity, ability, and aptitude.

3. In our exploration of what we like and don't, they offer valuable clues to identifying our heartfelt desires.

For these reasons, Seers decreed that all desires from the material to the spiritual be fulfilled.[20] In the ocean of life, we must first wade across egocentric desires for a glimmer of our spiritual nature.

Obsessive Egocentric Desires

When egocentric desires take us away from our core humane values, we become like the proverbial "bull in a china shop," rampaging and destroying our lives. I label these desires Obsessive Egocentric Desires or OED.

....

[20] Mundaka Upanishad 3.2.2.
kāmānyaḥ kāmayate manyamānaḥ sa kāmabhirjāyate tatra tatra | paryāptakāmasya kṛtātmanasvihaiva sarve pravilīyanti kāmāḥ | |

Seers refer to OED as insatiable desires that lead us toward excessive attachment, delusion, arrogance, anger and jealousy that result in pain and suffering[21]. They destroy all that we love and all that is beautiful in us and in the world. These are the desires spiritual texts allude to as an "enemy" on our spiritual path.

We reckon with OED from the moment we start giving undue primacy to egocentric desires without any consideration for others. At first, they may begin as a casual indulgence and soon grow to threaten our well-being. For example, my love for coffee can easily turn into an obsession for the same experience wherever I go, or the desire to invest in real estate can turn into an obsession leading one to cheat, or the consumption of alcohol for the desire to fit in can ultimately lead to addiction.

So here is what we need to know about desires. The energy of desire flows within us throughout the day in varying shades, some more potent than others. The way to recognize OED is in its manifestation in our feelings: lust, jealousy, greed and delusional thoughts of our own importance.

To give you an example, one of my schoolmates had to take financial responsibility for his family after he lost his father in his teens. What began as a necessity changed as he became older. He became obsessed with money and power. No doubt, he took care of his family financially and helped many of his friends. But he also cheated, grabbed and manipulated others. It soon came to a point where even when he helped someone, it was with the motive of leveraging their gratitude in the future.

---

[21] Bhagavad Gita. chapter 3:39, 2:62.

Today his OEDs reveal a man deeply troubled; always anxious about personal safety, suspicious of people's intentions, surrounding himself with lavish religious artifacts and wearing his superstitions like a cloak. **The same force that fulfilled his obsessive egoistic desire for wealth and power also led to alienation, fear, loneliness and the inability to love and recognize love in others.**

Obsessive egocentric desires essentially fall within three parameters:

1. They take us away from who we can be toward who we feel the need to be.

2. We break the five cardinal rules of non-violence (Ahimsa), truth (Satya), non-stealing (Asteya), moderation (brahmacharya) and non-grasping (Aparigraha).

3. We become victims of self-aggrandizement and have this delusional attitude that everything should serve us and everyone should adore us. Thus we disengage from meaningful relationships and feel ignored, isolated and disconnected from the world we have created around us.

Heartfelt Desire

Both shades of egoistic desires have in them the seed of heartfelt desires. **Heartfelt desires are a calling. They come from deep within us and manifest qualities of soul energy.** Think of them as a 'personal summons' or a "tap on the shoulder" to your potential and a calling to live your best life. Many times they surface, in our personal or professional life after some soul-searching, crisis, personal loss, or a mystical experience. At other times we manifest them in everyday quotidian activities like cooking, telling stories to children, caring for others, etc.

I offer you two examples that exemplify heartfelt desires. I share with you these portraits of desire so you can understand they are not necessarily earth-shattering but can manifest in simple ways in our everyday lives.

Twelve years ago my friend Sonja Sorenson, her three-year-old son Kayla and I were walking on the campus grounds at the University of Hawaii, Manoa campus. I was there for a semester as a visiting scholar in the Theater and Dance department. At that time Sonja lived with her family on a boat. That's right. The boat was her home. As we were chatting we came down a broad, linear stairwell of 15 steps with individual stair rise at about 6-7 inches. The broad structure was divided by a handrail. While we were down the third step on one side of the handrail I noticed her three-year-old son going down the steps on the other side of the handrail. In a moment of panic, I rushed to the other side. As I was bending down to take his hand, I momentarily turned to look at Sonja. I was surprised to find my friend smiling at me with amusement. "Kale lives on a boat. He knows how to balance himself," she said. And I said aloud, "But a 15-step flight of stairs? I don't think so!" Ignoring her indulging smile and giving in to my self-doubts, I stepped closer to the boy… 'Just in case…' I told myself. At every step, I kept a close watch on this little boy ready to save him from an imagined accident while he gleefully breezed down the stairs like a seasoned model on the ramp.

Sonja was absolutely right. She acted on a deep knowing, an intuition that Paulo Coelho describes as "An immersion of the soul into the universal current of life."[22] It was her heartfelt desire for her son to grow up believing in himself and without fear and so she subconsciously embraced those qualities herself. Such is the transformative power of heartfelt desires.

That was my first encounter and experience of the way of heartfelt desire. It made me realize the many times I had suppressed this voice within me as 'rubbish' because recognizing it meant I had to let go of my deeply guarded fears (of my ability mostly) and dare to follow my heart.

* * *

My grandmother was a super busy homemaker. Her time was divided among eight children, a demanding husband and extending hospitality to all those who came home. She got up at 4 a.m. every morning and went to bed at 9:30 p.m. She was on her feet all through the day attending to family and visitors.

But she created an oasis of time for herself every day very early in the morning. She made time for prayer, and reading from the scriptures. My mother can't remember a day she skipped this ritual. By evening, close to our bedtime, she would distill the essence of the scriptures in stories of bravery, truth and honor. She was a wonderful storyteller, who brought mythological stories to life and gave wings to our imagination.

My earliest memory of this was during the summer holidays when we visited her at our ancestral village at Dimili, a village

[22] Alchemist by Paulo Coelho, Kindle edition, page 90 of 195

situated in Vishakapatnam district in the state of Andhra Pradesh, south India. In the evenings while our mothers were busy clearing away remnants of dinner, we settled around our grandmother for our daily bedtime entertainment. On special occasions prompted by the weather, we would make our beds in the open courtyard space that connected the main door to the kitchen. There under the clear dark sky and shimmering stars we listened to her magical stories.

One night I needed to go to the bathroom in the middle of Krishna's adventures. I was petrified to walk down the unlit path to the bathroom (situated as a separate enclosure, on an open field, by the far end of the house). Grandma looked me in the eye and gently told me not to be scared because Krishna would follow me. She assured me He will always be where I am. By then I was so enthralled by His fantastical adventures, that I was confident Krishna would follow me to the bathroom and grab meandering snakes on the way. I didn't know then, but that was the day my grandmother unwittingly gave me the biggest gift of my life—a sense of belonging and connection to divine energy within me— not as existing outside in a temple or in the manner of performing rituals but as existing within me. Over the years, this innate sense of belonging helped me navigate very painful emotions.

Grandma chose to live from her heart. By doing this she lit all of her children's and grandchildren's lives from within. This may seem like a commonplace example, but underlying its simplicity is a profound teaching and the enduring legacy of heartfelt desires.

Such outcomes of heartfelt desires: Love, compassion, peace, truth, stability, empathy, courage, resonate with the energies of the universe. Therefore, the more we attend to egocentric desires and cultivate them, the deeper our experiences of our highest and noblest qualities will be, and the closer we will be to experiencing 'authentic empowerment.' [23]

The ripple effect, of each of us bringing forth the 'hidden treasures' of heartfelt desire, is beyond the scope of our ordinary imagination.

By definition, heartfelt desires fulfill three criteria:

> They are innate and unique to each of us. They are meaningful and thus add value to our lives. They are physically, mentally challenging, immersive, enjoyable and integrative. That is, they catalyze multiple interests in complementary ways. Every heartfelt desire is the coming together of multiple egocentric desires.

They spark creativity in unique ways and obviate notions such as 'it has already been done, so I won't do it.'

They tap into the three faculties of intelligence, emotional resilience and appropriate action. Because they speak to our deepest instincts, these desires align with how we think, feel and act in requisite measure. In Hindu mythology, the divine mother, Shakti, embodies these three energies as Jnāna shakti (Cognition), Icchā shakti (Emotion/desire) and Kriyā shakti (Action).

The path to heartfelt desires is filled with overwhelming challenges and obstacles. It will call for us to show up (rather than pretend 'all

[23] Gary Zhukov, in The Seat of The Soul, defines authentic empowerments as, " when the personality comes fully to serve the energy of its soul." kindle edition, p 15 of 332

is good'), reckon with our fears and self-doubts, navigate difficult emotions, and it will also require us to challenge prevailing cultural ideas and attitudes in ways we never imagined.

So if you are wondering, 'Why bother with heartfelt desires if life is going to be difficult, when it is much easier to just talk about spirituality, discuss/debate religious topics, and practice rituals', here is a reason:

When you give up on your desires, you give up the possibility of fulfilling a dream. As a consequence, you give power to fear. Fear will then block your heart from reaching out to you. Anger and frustration will build. This will create an unpleasant and unsafe environment for your loved ones who, by the way, are likely to follow your lead and do as you do

The three desires can be represented thus;

Fig.5. Three forces of desire

Zoom-in:

How Can You Identify Heartfelt Desires?

Identify heartfelt desires by exploring a range of activities that pique your curiosity, especially those that follow the three E-rules: Enjoyable, Engaging, and Enlightening.

Look into those activities that assimilate your core self and social self; what you enjoy doing, what engages and challenges your potential, and leads to greater knowledge. It must give you a sense of "one-pointed" focus or an experience of a "flow-state in which people are so involved in an activity that nothing else seems to matter; the experience is so enjoyable that people will continue to do it even at great cost, for the sheer sake of doing it." [24]

They must be activities that you can integrate into your daily routine. This may require you to organize your time and prioritize activities, so you can accommodate them around available time. I often found myself exhausted and frustrated with dance because I overcommitted. Under the pressure of time, I stopped enjoying my practice altogether, and worse, I felt burdened by it. So, prioritize activities that you want to learn more about, and give yourself enough time to practice.

To further assist you, I offer some guideposts below that will help you recognize how the three desires are expressed in daily life.

[24] Cikszentmihalyi. Flow: The Psychology of optimal experience p.4 of 304 Kindle.

I have found that labeling the desire underlying choices in the past transforms the way we choose, act, and behave today and tomorrow.

Guideposts to identifying desires

Obsessive Egocentric desires	Egocentric desire	Heart-centric desire	Field of potential/ divine/ soul energy
Driven by sensory longings and pleasures and centered on fulfilling selfish interests without consideration for another	Fulfills sensory and material longings without hurting another	Employs intelligence and power of discernment to act for the common good	Field of intelligence and wisdom
Driven by greed and hubris	Driven by a need for security, enjoying simple pleasures and expressing one's self	Driven to serve others and self	Field of generosity and contentment
Actions and behaviors focused to amass wealth and power	Actions are focused on enjoyable and meaningful activities	Actions and behaviors oriented toward things that hold value and meaning to self and others	Field of one-pointed focus
Takes you away from your core spiritual personality	Takes you toward your core spiritual personality while trying to integrate your inner and outer self	Integrates inner and outer self, harmoniously	Field of truth
Inability to understand any point of view other than one's own	Able to understand multiple views but accepts point of view that serves self-interest	Unifies diverse perspectives toward a common goal	Field of awareness

Obsessive Egocentric desires	Egocentric desire	Heart-centric desire	Field of potential/ divine/ soul energy
Expresses love that imprisons others by its demands	Expresses love that is conditional to personal likes and dislikes	Expresses love that liberates others	Field of love
Prompts you to accept a destructive, negative environment	Prompts you to accept what is good for you	Prompts you to transform your environment for positive outcomes	Field of joy
Encourages you to work for money, status, privilege	Encourages you to work for your well-being	Encourages you to find larger meaning in your work and invites you to time and again embark on your creative quests	Field of creative energy
Works alone, vies for opportunities and takes credit for achievements	Works with others to further one's interests and shares credit	Coordinates, collaborates and increases opportunities	Field of abundance
Manifests as resentment, jealousy, hubris, apathy, anger, suspicion and distrust	Manifests as kindness, generosity, gratitude, love and compassion	Manifests as love, joy and compassion	Field of equanimity

Emotional Well-being as a Clue

Our emotion, be it joy, an overall sense of well-being, excitement, compassion, love, generosity, dread, stress, anxiety, fear, frustration, insecurity, loneliness or any of the 87 emotions identified by Brené Brown[25] offers valuable clues to the nature of our desires.

---

[25] https://brenebrown.com/resources/atlas-of-the-heart-list-of-emotions/

You may have noticed that any activity that is too easy can be boring, or if too challenging and aggravating, is not enjoyable.

Heartfelt desires offer a good balance where the challenge is just right in relation to our skills. We know that because the joy of "flow" motivates us to learn more and relieves everyday stress and anxiety in us. These activities help us cultivate emotional resilience - to navigate painful emotions and find practical solutions to existing problems and transform our emotional landscape.

I present examples of such transformations below to help you get started. What activities make you feel that way?

Fig. 6. Transcending emotions

The process of looking into the forces of desire that operate within you is important so you are aware of what you need to be doing, have clear goals, and find a healthy balance between challenges in relation to your skills.

Another way to identify heartfelt desires lies in observing the power of Will.

As you ruminate on heartfelt desires, here is a quote by theologian Howard Thurman[26]:

> "Ask what makes you come alive, and go do it.
> Because what the world needs is people who have come alive."

A story of heartfelt desire

Suchint Murali loved her job in the corporate sector as the Director of HR in a multinational company. Helping people find jobs made her happy, and was aligned with her personality and motivations. Her job was demanding and she absolutely loved it!

28 years in this field, however, she found herself wondering if this was what she truly wanted for herself going forward. In as much as she loved her job she began to feel something was amiss. She often wondered if there was a more direct way of helping people. And perhaps she could make a bigger impact and have a more personally rewarding career if she ventured out on her own.

She quit her job to do some soul-searching.

[26] Howard Thurman as quoted in Gifts of Imperfection by Brené Brown. P 146-147

She reflected on her skill set: the ability to manage and connect with people, organize resources and her values: empathy, kindness, and connection, and determined that her priority was to serve people directly rather than through a corporation.

In the summer of 2019, soon after her father was fitted with a pacemaker she caught up with one of her close friends whose father was bedridden after an accidental fall. Over coffee, while sharing their concerns over their parents' health, they wondered how parents and children managed such situations when they were geographically away from one another, living so far apart that they could not give or arrange assistance in a timely manner. They imagined the worry and anguish of the children and the vulnerability of the parents. This triggered the idea of Sakhi4 Life, an organization that helps take care of parents whose children live abroad or out of state.

In October 2019, after a year and a half of soul-searching she along with two friends did a pilot launch, just to be sure this was the right choice. They officially incorporated the company in December of the same year.

When I met her in 2022, she told me of the challenges they faced daily and the many ways they catered to elderly clients, come rain, storm or sunshine. They are personally involved in services ranging from arranging for food and delivering it daily according to individual dietary requirements, speaking with doctors, driving clients to hospitals in the middle of the night, or just sitting and giving them company. During and after Covid their work has been all the more challenging for the mental health concerns they have had to address and support.

As physically exhausting and emotionally draining as her job is, Suchint says her heart is filled with love and gratitude for her family who supports her vision, for those who entrust their beloved parents and for the unquestioning trust of an ailing parent. At the end of a long, bone-weary day when clients hold her hands and express their gratitude with "God bless you" she feels richly rewarded and deeply fulfilled.

All Suchint wants now "Is to serve and honor the elderly in her community by giving them the loving care they need and dignity they deserve".

Now, the implicit assumption from Suchint's life is that she had a choice: to quit, to take time and to jump into a new venture. So what do you do if you have little or no choice due to social and financial constraints? Seers give us two options in such instances:

We can cultivate an attitude of service toward our current tasks instead of perceiving them as boring and frustrating.[27]

---

[27] Yoga Sutra of Patañjali, 2.33

In other words, we look at how our job is adding value to the community. The result of cultivating this type of attitude will add to our spiritual and emotional well-being. OR, we can look into what part of our job we like. Is it meeting new people, traveling, or any other? These are the egocentric desires you can tap into, that will lead you to your heartfelt desires.

WILL

The journey to fulfill a desire
Begins as a contractual promise
That honors the intellect of the mind and
the wisdom in the heart,
To complete a task for the well-being of the self and society. [28]

My husband, Sagar, is an avid hiker and by extension, a fitness nut. He exercises six days a week at our home gym. When he decides on what I think of as a pilgrimage to scale one of the higher altitude peaks or on a 2-3 week trek, he signs up with a group and then starts to prepare for it with a more-than-usual rigorous schedule.

Every day after work, following a light supper he heads off to the gym for a couple of hours or more of training. I have often seen him carrying a weighted backpack of about 50 pounds and walking on the treadmill at a 15 percent incline for extended periods of time. (Watching him is seeing a ritual of habits he formed around a goal). An experienced hiker he is more than aware of the strength and stamina he needs and the inherent risks

---

[28] Essence of Śiva Sankalpa Sūtra, chapter 34, verses 1-5,
http://www.onlineved.com/yajur-ved/

and unpredictability of high-altitude climbs. And he diligently prepares for them.

On the trek, he sleeps on uneven terrain and endures the challenges of inclement weather. What drives him to scale these mountains and remain steadfast in his regimen? The anticipation of revisiting the intense emotional experience of being one with nature, being among the mountains, standing at the summit in reverential silence amidst a higher power and soaking in the spectacular grandeur nature offers at such altitudes. The amount of time spent atop the mountain may be brief, but that intense experience of communion remains indelibly etched in his memory.

This is Will, a sacred contract, between our mind and soul energy to manifest our deepest aspirations. A contract that acknowledges our ability to complete a task with devotion.

On the flip side, we have our New Year resolutions that commonly vacillate within the first week or month. Up until five years ago, on every New Year's Eve I would excitedly make a resolution that I was certain would make me happier—toning my abs, maintaining a journal, reading 12 books a year, etc. They were certainly doable. Yet, by the end of January, my enthusiasm didn't go beyond shopping for a bright flowery journal and new exercise gear.

In 2018 things turned around for me. During an exceedingly busy year, I decided to restrict social engagements. There was always a dinner party or other engagement almost every weekend. I felt I had nothing in common with some of them. The worst part for me was the apprehension I felt days before the event, thinking of ways to cancel, and the guilt-tripping for having those thoughts. As emotionally draining as this was, I wanted above all to hunker down and do the things I really wanted to do. So, closer to December, the party month, I gave myself permission to politely refuse invitations unless they marked a celebration (birthday, anniversary, etc.) and accept only those of my close friends with whom I genuinely wanted to spend time. Unsurprisingly, this resolution stuck and I continue to honor it.

I say unsurprisingly because even as I made this resolve, I knew I would stick by it. So why did this work while the others utterly failed? I got my answer when I read an article by Kelly McGonigal where she says:

"Most New Year's resolutions almost always fail because they start from the assumption that who you are is not good enough, and reinforce the mistaken belief that your happiness depends on acquiring what you want"[29]:

This was an "Aha!" moment for me. It made me realize that my desire for flat abs came from social conditioning that a certain body type is beautiful and my desire to maintain a journal was not so much to put down ideas or observations, as I told myself, but more to serve the romantic notion of writing with a hot cup of coffee and gazing dreamily at a distant future. If it had genuinely been to put down ideas, a piece of serviette at a coffee shop (à la J.K Rowling) would

---

[29] Kelly McGonigle, How to create a Sankalpa, https://yogainternational.com/article/view/how-to-create-a-sankalpa

have sufficed. If I wanted to lose weight to be healthy and not to look good, it would have worked.

In identifying and manifesting heartfelt desires, an unbreakable Will fulfills the desires. Here is what seers say about Will.

Will as a Sacred Contract

Traditionally before the commencement of any auspicious activity, a resolve is undertaken summoning our ancestors and the innate wisdom of our mind and body. It is called a sankalpa in Sanskrit. **A sankalpa is a 'Declaration of Intent' to strengthen the will by invoking the collaborative power of intelligence (mind), and wisdom (heart).**

It is a solemn promise to ourselves, in which we articulate the time and place of the undertaking, invoke the energy of our ancestors to bless the undertaking and promise to fulfill it in accordance with righteous action and conduct for the prosperity, peace and happiness of the community to the best of our ability.

The prayers that follow summon the energy of our mind and heart. It goes like this:

> May I summon the energy that empowers the virtuous and wise, to this auspicious resolve.
>
> May the wisdom in my mind shine forth to fulfill this auspicious resolve.
>
> May my mind control the senses (from distractions) and be committed to this auspicious resolve.

May the mind that is aligned with the soul energy guide me on the path of righteousness for my well-being and for the welfare of humanity in fulfilling this auspicious resolve.

A sankalpa is thus a solemn promise we make to ourselves with deep faith in our ability and unwavering devotion to the task ahead. There is no room for doubts (Can I do it? Is it worth doing) or fear (What if I fail?) or shame (I am not good enough to do this).

Two Manifestations of Willpower

We invoke the power of Will in two ways: as a short-term promise or a long-term commitment

A Short-term Promise

In India, it is common to declare a resolve for many reasons. A few common resolves are fasting on certain days for the health of a loved one, eating vegetarian food and giving up smoking and alcohol before a pilgrimage, climbing up thousands of stairs to reach a temple and circumambulating its sanctum sanctorum a hundred and eight times. These are short-term testaments to our willpower and are called a Vrata (derived from the Sanskrit root Vri meaning 'to will.')

A Long-term Commitment

A Vrata can also be a lifelong commitment. This is a great vow or mahāvrata (maha meaning great), a spiritual practice that tests the limits of our physical and mental endurance. As a Mahāvrata, the power of Will is hailed by seers as the force behind every activity in the universe.[30]

History will always remember the indomitable Will of Mahatma Gandhi in fulfilling his heartfelt desire to see a nation free of foreign rule. He once said, "Strength does not come from physical capacity. It comes from an indomitable will."[31]

Dynamics of Will and Desire

The dynamics of Will and desire is a rather interesting interplay of forces. Any desire is only as strong or weak as its Will. Where Will is strong, desires are fulfilled, be they heartfelt, egocentric, or obsessive egocentric desires. By the Dharma of desires, an unkind thought or a harsh word is nothing but a lack of Will, as it requires a strong Will to control our thoughts, words, and actions.

In daily living, from the time we wake up till we go to bed, the strength of our will is tested along two paths: the path where we make choices that are beneficial and require hard work (Shreya); and the path where our choices are driven by what is quick, fun and pleasurable (Preya).[32] This again can be directed toward any of the three desires.

---

[30] Chandogya Upanishad 7.4.2
https://www.wisdomlib.org/hinduism/book/chandogya-upanishad-english/d/doc239349.html
[31] Eknath Easwaran, Essence of the Upanishads. p.116
[32] Kathopanishad verse 1.2.2. trans. by Swami Chinmayananda.
śreyaśca preyaśca manuṣyametastau samparītya vivinakti dhīraḥ | śreyo hi dhīro'bhipreyaso vṛṇīte preyo mando yogakṣemādvṛṇīte ||

The way to distinguish Will in heartfelt desires from Will in others is by checking into how uniformly strong our Will is in all areas of life. When we are on an exploration of heartfelt desires, we cultivate the will to be kind and loving to everybody. That is the nature of heartfelt desires. It gives us an experience of inter-being; that my well-being lies in the well-being of others. On the other hand, Will in obsessive egocentric desires is strong in one area and weak in another.

To give you an example of how Will fluctuates in obsessive egocentric desires, I share a poignant episode.

My friend Susan told me five years ago, "My biggest fear is that one day cops will knock on my door and tell me my son is dead." On November 2, 2020, Susan faced her worst nightmare when the cops knocked on her door.

It all began when her son Ben paid a visit to his dentist to have a wisdom tooth removed. Following the procedure he was given an opioid prescription for a few days. What began as a simple prescription drug for pain soon grew into a tragic addiction. In the years he was taking drugs he continued to work hard and get straight A's in college. His Will, so strong in meeting academic challenges was weak in overcoming addiction.

For years Ben tried to overcome his addiction. But in spite of his efforts and those of his family who took him to rehab facilities, attended family counseling and did everything possible to help him fight the disease, Ben's craving to feed the all-consuming desire for opioids outstripped his Will to recover.

Zoom-in

How Can You Strengthen Your Will?

Will is a measure of the depth of your desire.

From exploring egocentric desires, what desires consistently provide you with meaning and pleasure?

Once you have identified two or three desires frame your sankalpa and/or create a table of activities you enjoy doing. Initially, it is important to keep this where you can see it as a reminder until it becomes a habit.

Frame your saṅkalpa: Remember a saṅkalpa is a contract between what your heart desires and what your mind knows is possible. It is a promise you make to yourself not out of a perceived notion of shortcomings but rather out of acknowledging your skillset and the activities that you love to do.

I give you an example of my sankalpa:

I, *Anita Vallabh,* hereby commit to practicing meditation every *morning at 5:00 a.m.* because *meditation supports my commitment to slow down, be mindful of my choices and actions and cultivate patience.*

Anita Vallabh
January 1, 2023

You can similarly frame your sankalpa.

I *(name),* hereby commit to practicing meditation every *(when)* because *(why: How does it support you?)*

(Signature)
(Date)

Create a weekly Desire-Will Table: If you, like me, want to change a few other things besides your 'contract,' that will add to your well-being, like the number of cups of coffee you want to have or limit your TV time, you can create a Desire-Will table as an extension of your sankalpa. This will help you make the time to enjoy activities that are meaningful to you.

In the first column list your desire, in the second column list what is an optimal action plan for you, in the consecutive columns list the weekly frequency until these actions become a habit.

In the last column, I added emojis for fun, sparkles for trying and thumbs up for getting close to the optimal requirement. Make sure the optimal frequency is within a doable range so that it does not overwhelm you.

Desire	Optimal frequency	week 1	Will
Dance and Yoga	6 days/week	3 days	✨
Watching TV	2 hrs/day 6hrs/ weekend	2-3hrs/day 5-6 hrs/weekend	👍
Reduce cups of tea/coffee from four cups a day	1cup/day	1-2 -cups	👍

Review your list at the end of the day or the week, and think about how the small changes in your habits made you feel. Add or reduce time as you deem appropriate and note the activities that give you the most joy and those you want to learn more about. You will soon begin to see a glimmer of your heartfelt desire.

I offer you a poignant sentence by Nelson Mandela that tells us how he came into his heartfelt desire and framed the resolve to liberate his people[33]:

[33] Nelson Mandela. Long Walk to Freedom. Kindle edition. p.95 of 626

I had no epiphany, no singular revelation, no moment of truth, but a steady accumulation of a thousand slights, a thousand indignities, and a thousand unremembered moments produced in me an anger, a rebelliousness, a desire to fight the system that imprisoned my people. There was no particular day on which I said, "Henceforth I will devote myself to the liberation of my people; instead, I simply found myself doing so, and could not do otherwise."

A story of Will

In real-time sometimes a mahāvrata precedes self-inquiry, "How much can I do, what is my limit?"

My father-in-law, Sriramulu Vallabhajosyula, a retired commander of the Indian Navy at the time of writing this, is soon going to be a hundred years of age. He is perhaps the world's oldest and most decorated athlete with nine gold, five silver and two bronze medals at the Asian Masters Athletics Championships, as well as five gold and three silver medals at the World Masters Athletics Championships. He has won these medals in the 5,10 and 20 km speed-walking events. His last athletic meet was at age 96 when Covid put a pause on his dreams of competing. He is planning to go to the Philippines this summer for the next Asian Championships and also eagerly looking forward to competing in the 2024 World Masters Championships to be held in Sweden. He will be past 100 but does not believe that the figure needs to slow him down or reduce his will to remain physically fit and compete.

A few years ago he told me two things: The first was, "I want to see how much I can push the limits of my physical and mental endurance," and the other, "We are much more than who we think to be." In one he was voicing his desire, what he truly wants out of his life, and in the other, the outcome. What lies in between is a mahāvrata; an indomitable, sacred promise to tap into the immense potential of the body and mind.

During his many years in the Navy, he had always maintained a high level of physical fitness with running, rowing, racquet sports and sailing. He represented the Navy and at one time was also on the national sailing team. Since his retirement at age 60, however, he has kicked his fitness goals several notches higher. His daily morning routine begins at, believe it or not, 2:30 a.m. After some conditioning exercises, he hits the road, walking and running intermittently for anything between 10-20 km. He takes simple meals in small quantities, drinks plenty of fluids, and is in bed by 7:00 p.m.

At hundred he is just as willed and self-disciplined as he ever was. This is the power of Will when it sets about expressing a heartfelt desire during a lifetime.

ACTION

Actions performed as an offering
Are the "building blocks" to our highest destiny.

Three Forces of Action

In 1986 I was privileged to be part of a remarkable event when visiting my maternal grandmother in our village, Dimili (situated in the town of Yellamanchali, state of Andhra Pradesh). The villagers were informed by the village council that revered Guru and ascetic, Sri. Jeeyer Swamy was visiting to conduct a ritualistic offering (Yajña)[34] for the welfare of the community. Hundreds of women, men and children were called upon to participate in this event. Invitations were sent out to nearby villages. It was going to be a special community event.

The logistics of selecting the venue, renting a particular type of ceremonial awning, construction of the ritual enclosure and other details were discussed by an informal council of elders. Under their supervision and direction, the villagers were assigned some general responsibilities of cleaning and arranging. Specific jobs

---

[34] A vedic ritualistic tradition, conducted in front of a sacred fire.

of cooking, procuring groceries, and providing hospitality were given to select volunteers.

Preparations began in earnest.

Family members joined in to help one another. Information was shared and disseminated. Of course, there were frequent outbursts of disagreement. This was calmly dispelled by the village elders with a gentle reminder of the purpose of the upcoming event. In effect, everybody had to work around their personal histories of animosity and work together for something that would benefit them all.

So it was that within a couple of weeks, large ceremonial awnings were raised to prepare food and propitiatory offerings in large pots (even as they were fasting). Hospitality for nearby villagers attending the event was arranged. There was great energy and enthusiasm. Everybody spoke animatedly about the event and walked with a purpose in mind. In the evenings after a long day's work, everybody— the young and the elderly alike, sat around the chaupal (site of public discussion) to discuss the day's progress and the nitty-gritty of such an endeavor.

On the day of the Guru's visit, the entire village was aglow with a festive spirit; garlands of glowing orange and yellow marigolds and auspicious mango leaves strung across doorways of houses and along the site of the prayers, colorful Kolam designs graced the entryways, aroma of food wafted through the air and by evening everybody was dressed in their finest in eager anticipation of the renowned Guru.

From the time of his arrival, everybody took to their assigned tasks with great enthusiasm and camaraderie. Prayer chants reverberated across the village. After the prayers, food was served for the thousands of guests who arrived from near and far. Needless to say, the event was a big success, not only by the number of people who turned up for the event and participated in the Yajña (pronounced Yagya) but by the abiding sense of fulfillment that those involved in putting the event together experienced.

This is the kind of society seers must have envisioned. A society, where its members, like the instrumental ensemble of a philharmonic orchestra, perform actions aligned to their skill set and contribute toward the harmony and welfare of family, community and world.

At this juncture, it is worthwhile to recap the two main operating principles of Dharma of desires that frame our actions:

The first principle is to perform actions that fulfill both aspects of human life, the spiritual (what we truly desire), and social (fulfill our material desires and obligations toward our family and society).

The second principle is that every thought, word and deed is action; a play of cause (the thought or feeling with which you are doing something) and effect (how we manifest the thought in action and feel after the fact). This means, sitting on a comfortable bean bag watching TV while feeling sorry for your mom toiling away in the kitchen does not make you a compassionate person—acting on that thought and helping her makes you one. Thus compassion is an _act_ of kindness, and similarly, love is an _act_ of tenderness, trust is an _act_ of friendship, etc.

Now let's look at the three kinds of actions:

Karma, everyday duties and obligation

Akarma, selfless actions and,

Vikarma, prohibited actions.

Fig.7. Forces of Action

Karma: In the above example, all the villagers performed their assigned tasks with enthusiasm and experienced emotional fulfillment primarily because the tasks were aligned with their personalities. Those who enjoyed cooking were given the task of cooking, those who liked organizing were given the task of organizing, and so on. Thus, when they came together, they fulfilled a collective desire to help their community and served their own spiritual desire to serve a revered seer.

We experience this integration between the social and spiritual on a daily basis when we take care of our family, help a friend or serve our community.

Suppose you don't experience this integration because your job is not aligned with your skill set and aptitude. Naturally, you won't be looking forward to performing the necessary tasks. In such a scenario you work with the intention to pay the bills and take care of your family. You consider it a starting point to work your way up toward a job you truly want. These actions reflect your social values of self-accountability, duty and obligation and lay the groundwork for selfless actions. You then compensate for the lackluster job by taking up an engaging hobby or interest that is fun, enjoyable, and adds meaning as well as value to your life.

Akarma is the action performed without the expectation of any kind of reward. These actions are aligned with spiritual values and heartfelt desires.

Under this category are also those actions performed with the intention of serving a higher altar, be it family, community, or environment **without hankering for acknowledgment or monetary reward or ownership**. At the 'heart' of such action lies the essence of Karma Yoga[35] (the path of action): **perform the service and surrender the ego.**

We practice Akarma every day. When we give up our place in a queue for another, or our seat on a bus, or we take some food

---

[35] Bhagavad Gita chapter 5

to our neighbor who is in isolation for Covid, we set in motion future karmic patterns. It may be that in the past this neighbor ran her car over your lawn or ignored your repeated calls. But in extending help in their time of need, we are shaping our destiny as well as theirs in ways that enrich our well-being. These actions that we perform out of an abiding sense of community, love, and compassion for another are Akarma.

Most often, however, we don't think about them as 'higher order' actions because these are everyday actions. But if we ask ourselves why we cook or clean or work every day, why we give up our place in a long queue, why we take care of our parents, our everyday actions take on enchanting hues.

For example, I cook every day. At one time I read about intentional cooking. Curious, I decided to put that into practice. I asked myself why I cook every day. I was surprised at the answer that came back to me. I cook every day for the health and well-being of my family and myself. Now, to give you a better perspective. I do simple cooking, twice a day. Normally around that cooking, there is some drama 'Oh, the time it takes!' 'I am out of this vegetable!' etc.,—it is a chore to be done away with.

Bringing awareness of intention showed me a way out of this rather woebegone attitude. Where I would get exasperated by the amount of time it took to cut vegetables, I now actually enjoyed the process. Cooking made me feel responsible for my family. It made me acknowledge the significance of my responsibility. This strengthens my will and motivates learning to cook a variety of cuisines (thanks to our friends on YouTube).

The two values, responsibility, and family are in line with the top five values I hold sacred, the other three being (in case you are wondering) love, integrity, and friendship. Even now, every time I feel a sense of frustration, I recall my intention. It feels like the energy behind our intention, a reminder of "why" we are doing, what we are good at, or what we truly want for ourselves, gives us the motivation to act and to be consistent with it.

Within the DWAD framework, whether actions are Karma or Akarma they should be **intentional**: well-considered and purpose-oriented, and **integrated**: aligned to our spiritual and social self.

The third kind is prohibited actions **(Vikarma).**

A harsh word, an angry thought, or a physical push are all prohibited actions. When we think about it, every thought is a subtle form of action. It is as if our thoughts are a dress rehearsal for what is soon to be expressed on the stage of life. Once expressed these actions leave their mark on us as much or more than they do on others because they are out of sync with our innate desires for love, peace, and joy.

Every time we say something harsh it irreparably fractures our relationship, as much as we may apologize later. Such words begin as a thought that often arises from fear, greed, anger or frustration. Often when we observe another's phenomenal rise, say in the field of music, we may aspire for the trappings of their success (by a measure of wealth and power) and entirely miss the point that their career is aligned with their personality. In every failure, instead of anger and frustration, they cultivate courage and emotional resilience to navigate through difficult situations and move forward. In every success, they tap into the next desire and rise higher. Now if we were to emulate them out of our shared love for music, and a career in music is not aligned with our personality, every step would feel like an uphill task and failure would take an emotional toll on our well-being. In such a scenario it is best to take up music as an enjoyable and meaningful hobby. If not, we fall into a vortex of pain, hurting others and ourselves and create a toxic environment of fear, intimidation, manipulation, humiliation, shame and retribution for the people we love the most.

Hence the Bhagavad Gita[36] proclaims that it is better to do a job aligned to your personality with enthusiasm, fortitude, and right intention, rather than strive to do another's job.

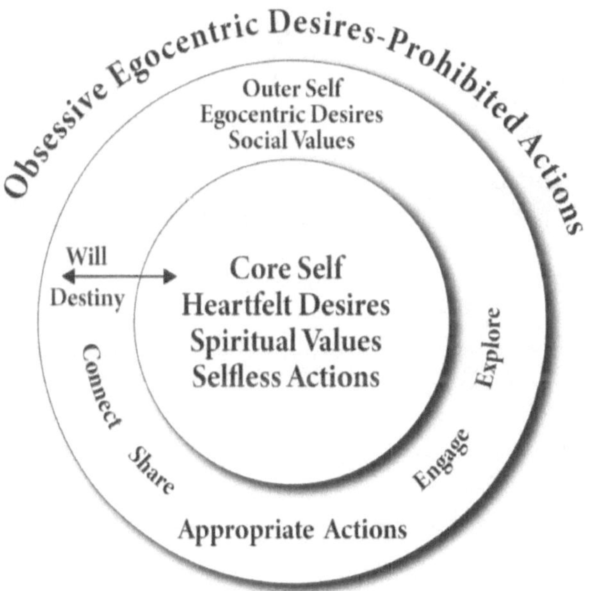

Fig 8. Desire, Will, and Action Dynamics

[36] Bhagavad Gita. 18.47: śhreyān swa-dharmo viguṇaḥ para-dharmāt sv-anuṣhṭhitātsvabhāva-niyataṁ karma kurvan nāpnoti kilbiṣham

We can correlate how we feel about our lives today by looking at our desire, the will that strengthened the desire and the action and behavior it led to. In a forest of infinite desires, prohibited actions reflect obsessive egocentric desires when they operate within the darkness of insatiable desires with no regard for spiritual or social values. Appropriate actions reflect egocentric desires when they are directed toward fulfilling meaningful desires to make a clearing, so the light of the sun illumines our life. Selfless actions reflect heartfelt desires, unafraid of heavy odds and the many ups and downs, and illumine the harmony between our core spiritual self and outer social self.

To summarize, I quote Mahatma Gandhi[37]:

> Your beliefs become your thoughts,
> Your thoughts become your words,
> Your words become your actions,
> Your actions become your habits,
> Your habits become your values,
> Your values become your destiny.

[37] Taken from goodreads.com

Zoom-in:

How to Make Ethical Decisions And Take Moral Actions?

I offer three choices, include them as appropriate:

1. **Form or be a part of a collective or what seers called, Sahṛdaya (meaning, in sync with your heart, in Sanskrit).**

   Actions, be it in your thinking, words or behavior, indicate the depth of desires, and strength of will, and move you forward toward your highest destiny. Seers say, these (thoughts, words and behavior) are influenced by the company we keep. When we are with opinionated people, we agree with what they are saying. When we are with agitated people, we participate in their agitation. Conversely, when we are in the presence of compassionate people, we practice compassion.

   Hence they suggest we either form or be a part of Sahṛdaya, a collective of people who share your desires and values, who have your best interests at heart, who hold you accountable, whom you implicitly trust and to whom you will commit the same values.

2. **Track your responses to challenging experiences.**

   The path to our highest destiny is challenging. It will require you to navigate difficult emotions—of failure, missteps, pain and adversity. Ruminate on your actions while confronting such experiences and reflect on the underlying desires and virtues that motivated the action. Were your actions selfish or selfless? Were you driven by courage or cowardice? Did you walk away thinking,

"Ignorance is bliss," or rise up to the challenge of learning? Did the experience make you more resilient?

Here are some examples of such experiences and two possible ways we respond to them. Create a similar table of an experience in one column and your response in another.

Experience	Response 1	Response 2
Failure	Evaluate, reset and move on to accomplish heartfelt desires	Hide in fear, repress emotions and give in to feelings of shame and inadequacy
Missteps	Take accountability	Blame others
Pain	Share feelings and come out of the darkness with hope in our hearts	Bully and be angry at others
Adversity	Identify key takeaways from the experience and remain steadfast to our duty	Give up and move on to the next big idea every time we face an obstacle

3. **Practice making ethical decisions and taking moral actions.**

To guide you on your rightful path, seers listed 10 guidelines.[38] They were laid down as mandated 'law' (not as an optional choice) and formed the bedrock on which heartfelt desires are experienced, shaped, and nurtured. I list the 10 guidelines, interpret what they mean and how we can cultivate them.

Reflect on the intention (why) and motivations (what drove the action) behind your action and check them against the 10 guidelines offered below:

---

[38] Ganganatha Jha, Manusmriti with the Commentary of Medhatithi Verse 6.92 https://www.wisdomlib.org.

Ethical and moral actions	What they mean	How to cultivate them
1. Fortitude	It means staying on course when the going gets tough, and having the courage to follow your heart	Recall your statement of Will (sankalpa) to mind, with faith in your heart and devotion to the task to keep yourself going
2. Forgiveness (yourself and others)	Looking at past unpleasant mistakes, failures, regrets and painful experiences as valuable teachings	Practice compassion for self and others.
3. Self-control	Doing one's duty without being carried away by what "looks" good to others, not being influenced by other people's opinions and attitudes and indulging in wrongful/hurtful behavior	Let go of self-doubts and feelings of powerlessness. Learn to say "no" without fear of alienation
4. Non-stealing	Non-stealing means not grabbing or taking away from others. It means not appropriating credit for others' work or conniving to steal somebody's belonging	Practice generosity and contentment
5. Purity	Clarity in thinking, speaking and action unblemished by negative thoughts.	Cleanse yourself of six "contaminating" emotions; obsessive desires, anger, greed, delusion, arrogance, and envy.
6. Control of the Sense-organs	Managing sensory cravings	Practice moderation and cultivate "freedom from dependencies and cravings."
7. Discrimination	Being able to decipher right and wrong actions and behaviors.	Explore your choices, make informed decisions and take rightful action. Choose to be loving, and respectful of diverse views and attitudes.
8. Knowledge	In-depth learning and knowing of self, others and worldly matters	Listen, observe, think, read, research, learn and practice
9. Truthfulness	To think, speak and act with integrity.	Cultivate openness to the truth of the present moment and set yourself an honesty bar. Be aware of the influence of past experiences and conditioned thinking on your perception of truth.
10. Patience	Expression of peace and love within ourselves	Recognize impatience and aggression in your behavior, observe the consequences of your anger/irritation on your body, breath and relationships, slow down and cultivate an expansive attitude toward wants, likes and dislikes

A Story of Desire, Will, and Action

One of my oldest and dearest friends is Sanjay Rao Chaganti. He is the only person whom I have observed closely who has curated his calling by consciously bringing together his desires and skill sets. From my standpoint he has always infused everything he did, be it at work, at a party, or at home, with his brand of tongue-in-cheek and self-deprecating humor. I vividly remember his love for the stage, the spotlight, the audience, the applause…everything. He just reveled in the connection he established with his audience. This is the trademark of Sanjay.

Unsurprisingly, after his Master of Arts degree in communications he landed a job at one of the largest non-governmental organizations, PSI (Population Services International). Here, for 20 years he leveraged his communication skills to engage, motivate, entertain and inspire people from conservative cultural backgrounds and impoverished communities across Africa and Asia. He loved his job. It allowed him to savor his personal identity of wanting to make people happy with his social identity of educating and positively impacting people's lives. Life was good.

That is, until 2006.

Over a two-year period starting in 2006, Sanjay experienced two profound personal and professional setbacks that sent him on a downward spiral. The sudden and untimely loss of a friend, and two work-related incidents made him question life, its unpredictability, and his place in it. When a sponsor called off funds for a project, it was his responsibility to inform his team of four hundred co-workers (who looked to him for leadership), that they were out of jobs, and also bear the burden of its outcome on those they served. He woke up to the fact that his professional life was directed by powers beyond his influence.

Disheartened, he took time off to introspect. Alone, he struggled to articulate his emotions. He felt disconnected from his family. He could not articulate the depth of his despair, and 'couldn't recognize the darkness in the sky for the passing clouds'.

In 2011, he came upon Yoga Studio 136.1 (named for the frequency of OM). In his teacher Santanu, he found someone he could relate to, and soon became part of a 'Sangha' (community of like-minded seekers). Santanu suggested a trip to the Bihar School of Yoga. There, in a remote, nondescript region of Munger, Bihar (Eastern India) he experienced the mind component of Raja Yoga practice for the first time. He had a vague sense that he was in the vicinity of what he was looking for.

Then in early 2014, an advertisement for a teacher training program for 'Heal Your Life' caught his attention. Following his inner voice, he attended the training. This opened a whole new world for him. Over the next 18 months, he followed his heart, indulged his curiosity and traveled across continents to seek knowledge related to various topics ranging from Emotional Intelligence, Coaching, Non-Violent Communication, and Raja Yoga. Gradually he developed a framework that integrated his personal life experiences with the transformational practices and time-tested wisdom of ancient cultures.

In late 2015 he quit his job, decided to honor his inner voice, and dove into uncharted waters as an independent coach and workshop facilitator. Eight years into manifesting his heartfelt desire, Sanjay is happy to have leveraged the 'lows' in his life. They enabled him to create for others "opportunities for structured introspection toward cultivating fulfilling lives".

Now, to understand the magnitude of Sanjay's decision, we need to understand the prevailing attitude toward emotional well-being in India. First of all emotional coaching is not looked upon as a real or worthy 'job'. Secondly, his role is commonly facilitated by friends and family, regardless of the seriousness of underlying issues. Also, from the standpoint of a person who needs help, any whisper of seeking professional help, comes with the heavy baggage of guilt and shame to the person and his family.

In this socio-cultural milieu, Sanjay's decision to nurture the emotional well-being of his clients is just as laudable as the courage it takes for sensitive, high achievers like Dr. Nayanjeet Chaudhury (Medical doctor and Director at

Ramaiah International Center for Public Health Innovations)[39] to approach Sanjay and seek help. Nayanjeet credits Sanjay for 'holding a mirror' to his thought process, and in helping him acknowledge, unravel and overcome emotional complexities. Today, Nayanjeet finds joy and meaning in nurturing young minds in the domain of Public Health.

The strategies Sanjay employed will work for anyone who knows what they desire in life, is aware of their skill set, and is open to learning, exploring, and experimenting with a wide range of opportunities that come up along the path of desires. He continues to advance his work by learning and exploring, as much out of personal curiosity (what will I learn?) as for professional reasons (how can I help others with this learning?). He says, "The connecting and learning journey is itself fulfilling for me. All I truly want is to feel a deep sense of contentment, emanate positivity, love, abundance, and bring joy to the world."

For anyone else, being an emotional coach in a traditional society such as in South India may seem a daunting challenge. For Sanjay, it felt 'just right'[40].

---

[39] To know about Dr. Nayanjeet's work visit: https://www.RICPHI.org

[40] To know more about Sanjay Rao Chaganti visit: https://www.sanjaychaganti.com/about-me

DESTINY

What do you truly want your life to look like?
Your answer, is the destiny that awaits you.

Demystifying Destiny and Highest Destiny

Over the years of researching for this book and "me-searching", a notion of destiny that came up commonly was that it is predetermined. When you hold that against a wisdom template that says 'you shape your destiny,' the contradiction is obvious.

In this section, I wish to unpack what destiny really means and the two main reasons for this confusion. I do this with the intention to help you steward your life in the direction you want with a clear understanding of what destiny means.

The basis of confusion lies first, in the language itself; trying to grasp its meaning encrypted in Sanskrit by looking through the lens of an English term derived from Latin.

The English word destiny comes from the Latin "destinaire», meaning "make firm, establish[41]"

It implies our destiny is predetermined, already established.

---

[41] https://www.etymonline.com/word/destiny

In Sanskrit, seers use the term "Abhisampad" meaning "to become, obtain,"[42] It implies we create and shape our destiny. Destiny then is the dynamic process of an array of forces; desire, Will, and action.

Secondly, within its usage in Sanskrit, there is uncertainty between destiny and highest destiny.

Let's clarify this:

Destiny is the life we consciously or subconsciously shape by our desires, the strength of Will, and the force of action.

The highest destiny is the one we consciously strive toward, to shape the life we truly want for ourselves. This means we cultivate heartfelt desires, fortify our Will toward the desire and choose selfless actions. The objective is to fulfill all desires until there are no more.[43]

Within the realm of this understanding, we are shown two paths:

One path requires seekers to renounce worldly desires as well as attachments, and undertake a yogic path of austerity and meditation to cultivate "altered states of awareness"[44] for an experience of "spiritual liberation."

....

[42] M. Monier-Williams. A Sanskrit English Dictionary. Edited and revised by Pandit Ishwar Chandra, p.1711

[43] Eight Upanishads with commentary of Sankaracharya, trans. By Swami Gambhirananda, Advaita Ashrama, Kolkata 2016 p.154

kāmānyaḥ kāmayate manyamānaḥ sa kāmabhirjāyate tatra tatra |
paryāptakāmasya kṛtātmanasvihaiva sarve pravilīyanti kāmāḥ || 2 ||

[44] Gerald James Larson, Ram Shankar Bhattacharya. Encyclopedia of Indian Philosophies. Vol.XII p. 30

The other path requires that we immerse ourselves in a "disciplined work" (within ordinary awareness) toward an experience of joy, beauty, love, transcendence and abundance.

The path of Yoga referred to in this book focuses on the second path. It involves consciously bringing our awareness and focus into activities and practices that give us joy, add meaning and purpose to our lives, and help us shape the life we truly want for ourselves.

Naturally, the highest destiny will then mean different things to people across the socio-economic spectrum. For example, when I asked Jyothy a flower vendor, what she ultimately wanted in her life, she said "I want to live without abuse, without financial debt and I want my children to get a good education and a job." Similarly Arun, a vegetable vendor selling fresh produce under a temporary shack, wanted to own a shop. Each of the 40 students (undergraduates and graduates) who attended my workshop in Chennai wanted very different things out of their lives.

What I came to understand is that however differently we may want to shape our lives depending on our age, personality, and social and cultural circumstances, we are united by a common desire:

To create a space within ourselves where anxieties, fears, and self-doubts, as well as worldly burdens fall away, where we are free of dependency and where we are joyful and at peace with ourselves and the world around us.

This then is our highest destiny. So what does a life moving toward our highest destiny really look like in our day-to-day living? It means:

Getting up in the morning with enthusiasm for what lies ahead and the fortitude to address challenges in the spirit

of thinking: Life is a gift, how may I serve this best given my talents and resources?" It is going to bed with a prayer of gratitude for what has been achieved and thinking: I left some things undone and made some mistakes today, but my perceived shortcomings do not take away from my spiritual truth that I am love, intelligence and bliss.

This spirit of thinking of life as a gift and our unique talents as endowments to be shared for the well-being of others is spiritual living. Nowhere is this more evident than in the lives of those who leave behind a lasting legacy and inspire others on their journey.

I share with you one such story.

A Story of manifesting desires with an indomitable Will, and ethical and moral actions toward the highest destiny.

A million villagers across 50 villages in and around Yelamanchili district of Visakhapatnam, situated in the south of India go to bed knowing they will wake up to a job, their children will go to school, wear clean, well-made clothes, eat nutritious, homegrown food, and ingest clean drinking water from nearby bore wells. This is no mean feat given that 50 years ago any visitor to any one of those villages would have confronted a hostile, barren land bereft of water and people worn by economic poverty. Children would have had to walk five miles each way to reach the nearest school. Women would have had to walk a mile or so to draw water from the nearest well. Men would have had to rely on daily wages with their employment subjective to the whims of local politicians and wealthy merchants.

All this changed because of the desire of one man, Dr. Parameshwara Rao, who intuited that his future lay in his ancestral village of Dimili, near Yelamanchili. It was here that as a child he happened to come across two illiterate old men deliberating upon the Bhagavad Gita and Bhagavata Purana (canonical texts of Hindu wisdom). This image, or rather, the irony of spiritual discussion amidst economic poverty, seared into his memory. It would gain potency in the years to come.

Meanwhile as an adult, after completing his undergraduate studies in India, he set out to do a Ph.D. in nuclear physics at Pennsylvania State University, USA. He pursued this line of education at the behest of his father even though, at heart, he wished to serve the people in his ancestral village. During this time the irony of his childhood memory was never lost in him. Deep down he knew that the collective wisdom of the villagers could be tapped for their own social and economic upliftment. He fervently wanted to be the catalyst, or, as he would later call, 'a head clerk' of an integrated rural program, for the villagers. And so, after completing his Ph.D. he turned down an offer of assistant professorship at the university as well as a high-paying job at India's Atomic Energy Establishment to return to the village and fulfill his heartfelt desire.

In 1968 on the day of Mahatma Gandhi's birthday, against the hardship of winning the trust of the villagers and wealthy prospective donors, getting permission from politicians, and a not-so-happy nod of consent from his father, he opened the Dimili High School. This was no ordinary, academically oriented school. Besides academics, farming, carpentry, electric and plumbing work, toy making and even the clothes they wore—from picking cotton, transforming the raw cotton to cloth by spinning and weaving to tailoring—formed an essential part of their curriculum.

This was just the beginning.

Soon after, his once-unrelenting father gave him the money to start a hospital in the family name. Thus was born The Bhagavatula Charitable Trust (BCT) and under its aegis, many programs for women were initiated for their health and economic independence. What began as a desire to motivate villagers to actively participate in their own economic well-being subsequently opened venues for other co-dependent, integrated rural development programs[45].

As hard and challenging as each task was, the manner in which he went about initiating new projects and navigating difficulties, seemed effortless. It was as though with the stroke of a brush he was fulfilling a whole spectrum of heartfelt desires; educating and skill training, promoting creative arts, creating spaces for employment, rehabilitating people with disabilities, and improving agricultural outcomes for farmers. To him, an integrated approach was the only way to improve lives everywhere.

For every challenge that came his way, he contemplated deeply within himself to find resolutions to negotiate between

---

[45] For more details refer: https://www.bctindia.org

local politicians and village leaders and to forge a path that would benefit all the villagers, never losing hope in the face of adversity or undermining the wisdom of the elderly. Whether it was bringing water to the villagers, converting dry hills to cultivable land, or rehabilitation programs for the physically challenged, he always engaged the local people in the decision-making process, seeking counsel from the elderly and motivating the young.

Growing up, I spent every summer holiday in this village, interacting with the villagers, enjoying delicious farm-fresh food, and basking in the reflected love and respect the villagers had for my uncle, Dr. Parmeshwar Rao, and his brother Srinivasa Rao who stood by him through the years.

Then in 2007 under the aegis of BCT, I conducted dance workshops to revive their folk art tradition (dance and music) at Dimili High School. For this, we invited artistes-turned-agricultural laborers to teach their art. Every evening after a hard day's labor in the fields, the artistes came to teach at the school. Over the week it became abundantly clear that the process of reviving folk arts was as much a rejuvenating experience for the teachers as it was a fun learning experience for the students. In the 10 days I was there, I noticed that it forged new and meaningful connections between them.

The following year, my cousin Ramesh (Parameshwar Rao's son) reported fewer incidences of domestic violence. To my complete surprise, I was told that keeping the men engaged in the evenings, meant there was no time to indulge in drinking alcohol and therefore lesser incidence of domestic violence.

This was my first hands-on experience with the ripple effect of heartfelt desires. One can only imagine the impact of the three hundred other educational programs that take place throughout the year at BCT.

In 2012 after a serious health setback, he wrote a note thanking his family and in his words "for allowing me to share this life with you all. With you, I was blessed to lead a life of my choice." My uncle passed away in 2019. In the last few weeks of his life, as he lay in the hospital he confided to Ramesh that his only prayer to God now was to either give him the energy to continue serving his people or allow his soul to depart this body in peace.

Till the end of his life, Dr. Parmeshwar Rao wholeheartedly believed in the power of India's villages. He had absolute faith in the common-sense wisdom of its people. Awards and accolades meant nothing if they did not bring in much-needed governmental support to the villagers. All he truly wanted was to help villagers be self-sufficient, to take an active part in the electoral process and for every child to have an academic and as well as skill-based education.

Ramesh, the torch bearer of the same ideals and aspirations tells me, his father's often quoted phrase was 'It would take a genius to keep India poor.'

Dr. Parameshwara Rao's legacy has helped shape the destiny of millions in the villages in Andhra Pradesh.

This is the life he willingly chose, and the highest destiny he consciously shaped.

Dynamics of Desire, Will, Action. and Destiny

To summarize our experience of the DWAD template I offer you an illustration of its flow toward our highest destiny.

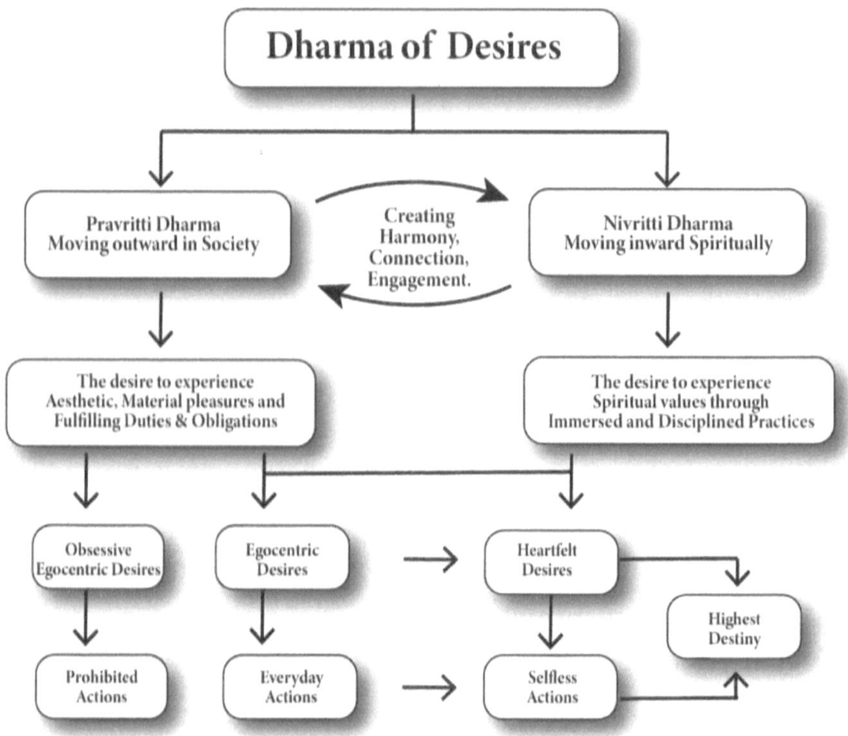

Fig.10 Dharma of desires.

Zoom-in

What do you truly want out of your life?

Create your vision board.

I offer you my vision board for this book project and this is how it looked:

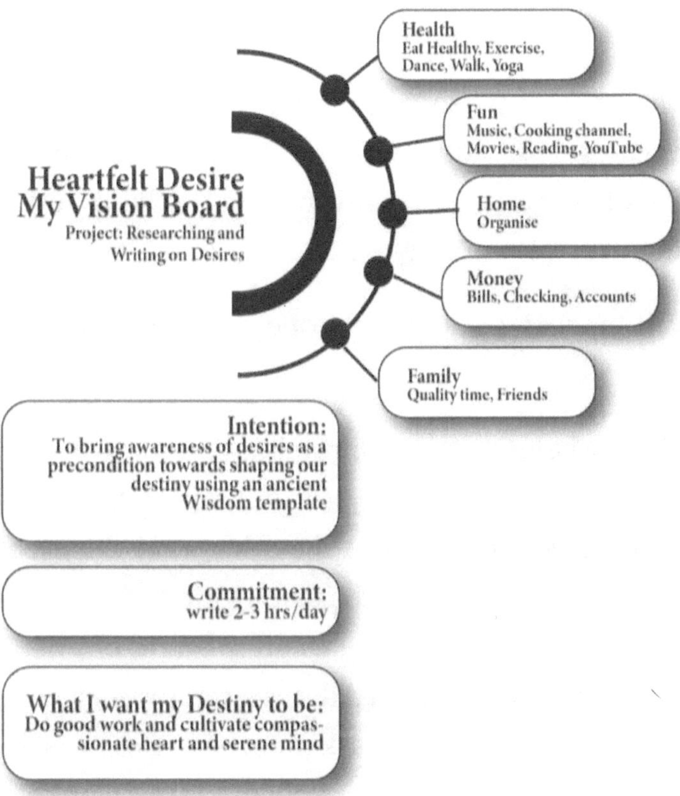

Fig 11. Vision board

Now that you have an overview of what to expect and what to avoid, you have an idea of the desires that are meaningful to you, you have a vision statement and the actions to take, I invite you to create a vision board, for short-term projects or long-term objectives, to bring together the DWAD variables in one place. Creating your vision board makes it possible in tangible ways to manifest them. It is a great way to stay focused and track your progression. If it serves your project to mark timelines and milestones, feel free to add it to your board. Enliven your project with stickers and colorful stationery, if you love stationery as I do.

I highly recommend you keep checking in on this board to encourage you to stay on track.

Depending on your personal choice, say you are into journaling, you can categorize your daily/weekly DWAD musings into two different sections; going inward, and moving forward and correlating the two regularly

Here is an inspiring quote from one of the greatest physicists ever: [46]

"A human being," wrote Einstein, "is a part of the whole, called by us 'Universe', a part limited in time and space. He experiences himself, his thoughts, and (his) feelings as something separated from the rest—a kind of optical delusion of his consciousness. This delusion is a kind of prison for us, restricting us to our personal desires and to affection for a few persons nearest to us. Our task must be to free ourselves from this prison by widening our circle of compassion to embrace all living creatures and the whole of nature in its beauty. Nobody is able to achieve this completely, but the striving for such achievement is in itself a part of the liberation and a foundation for inner security."

[46] The Einstein Papers. A Man of Many Parts, by Walter Sullivan, March 29, 1972

PART 4

. . . .

MOVE FORWARD AND R.I.S.E

*As flowing rivers become one with the
ocean
Giving up name and form,
So does the illumined soul, freed from name
and form,
Merge with the divine energy, to its highest
destiny.*

Muṇḍaka Upanishad 3.2.8

CREATIVE PROCESS TO HEARTFELT DESIRES

At the heart of the wisdom of seers is a universal message:

We all want to live in a beautiful world, a world where there is love, respect, empathy and kindness. Nobody wishes for hatred, divisiveness, cynicism, and violence. Yet we find ourselves in such a world. And each of us is individually responsible. We either shaped or allowed ourselves to be guided by narratives—of dissent creating divisiveness, of intolerance rendering hate, and rage instigating violence, in our thoughts, words, and actions. There is an apparent disharmony in the world we want to live in and the world we have created.

If we made such a world possible, we certainly can create "the more beautiful world" our hearts desire. We can start the work by first creating a space of love, respect, empathy and kindness within ourselves. The light it sparks within us will help us shine brighter as individuals, and soon enough, as an ecosystem.

I learned just how to begin the process as I was heading back home from the Nataraja temple at Chidambaram (refer to part 1) where my exploration of desires began.

Along the East Coast Road, within modestly-built enclosures, I came upon sculptures of gods, goddesses, seers and animals, chiseled down to their finest, harmonious, and most intricate detail. Beside these completed sculptures were piles of discarded stone chips in various shapes and shades.

I stopped by a shop with the signage 'Selva Vinayagar Sculptures,' and struck up a conversation with the sculptor and owner, Mr. Rukmangathan. Out of curiosity, I asked him about his artistic process.

He replied:

"I wake up every morning at 4:00 a.m. I take a shower and then say my prayers asking for God's benevolence in the task ahead and forgiveness for unseen errors. Prayers are an important part of the process. They give me the energy to focus. I then have a light breakfast and begin my work. If it is a commissioned work, I mark the requested dimensions with a pencil on the slab of stone. From there on I focus only on the vision I see in the stone and chip away all that is not part of that vision. On the rare occasions that I have the time, I sculpt the image that comes from deep within me."

And then as I looked closely I noticed that his name was not engraved on the sculptures. When I asked him about it, he said he was simply following a tradition set by his father and grandfather before him. "We cannot leave a name on a divine work of art and claim, I did it. Anything we create is divine and belongs to the gods, we cannot own it."

Spoken simply from his heart, his artistic process holds a mirror to the creative process in shaping our heartfelt desires as well.

This is how the creative process unfolded in my life:

I moved to the US over 10 years ago from India. As an immigrant, I felt a deep schism within—as if I belonged neither to my home country nor to my adopted one. Intellectually I knew what Spiritual texts proclaim—that we belong to ourselves. But in my heart, I didn't feel that way at all. I felt lost and fragmented like I neither belonged to Chennai nor Boston. And I wanted to feel belonged.

Without being fully aware of 'what' and 'why,' during my visits, I started to leverage the unique opportunities the social and cultural circumstances the two places provided to hone my skill set (dancer, social researcher, and teacher), and forge connections with friends and family. While in Chennai, I made use of the resources available by taking one-on-one Yoga lessons at the famed Krishnamacharya Yoga Mandiram, watching dance performances, spending time with my teachers discussing dance and philosophy, teaching at the university, and giving dance lessons. In Boston, I put down in writing ideas for further study and research, and I spent time with my family and step-grandchildren. Without quite realizing it I was harmonizing my core spiritual self with my outer social self.

As I was beginning to enjoy my experiences in both places, I realized there was limited time to do all the things I wanted to do. I needed to create time for myself. That is when my chipping-away process began.

I chose to be with people who valued my time and whose time I valued. It meant spending time with only those friends and relatives with whom I shared a trusting relationship and with whom I could have meaningful conversations. The people I stopped engaging with were those who gossiped (who couldn't wait to tell me what was going on in other people's lives), those who were more interested in their phones and the naysayers and doomsayers whom I found to be an emotional drain on my being. I let go of what others felt about me and I let go of trying to please people. As a result, I had more time to be with people I truly cared about and to do things that were meaningful, like being available for the people I loved in times of need.

From my experience, I can say to you that overall, the "chipping-away" process allows us to hit the pause button, enjoy the beauty, feel love and be inspired. It helps us cultivate self-awareness, envision what we truly want, instill self-discipline; work toward creating the life we truly want, and experience self-transcendence: be present in the moments where nothing but the beauty and joy in what we are doing or witnessing exists. In such experiences we R.I.S.E[47].

R. I. S. E. refers to rising upwards on our well-being quotient and also serves as an acronym for the transformational changes that will occur synchronously within four aspects of your personality: Relational, Intellectual, Spiritual, and Emotional.

---

[47] Inspired by S.P.I.R.E model of "whole person well-being" by the Wholebeing Insititute. *https://wholebeinginstitute.com*

Here is a graphical representation:

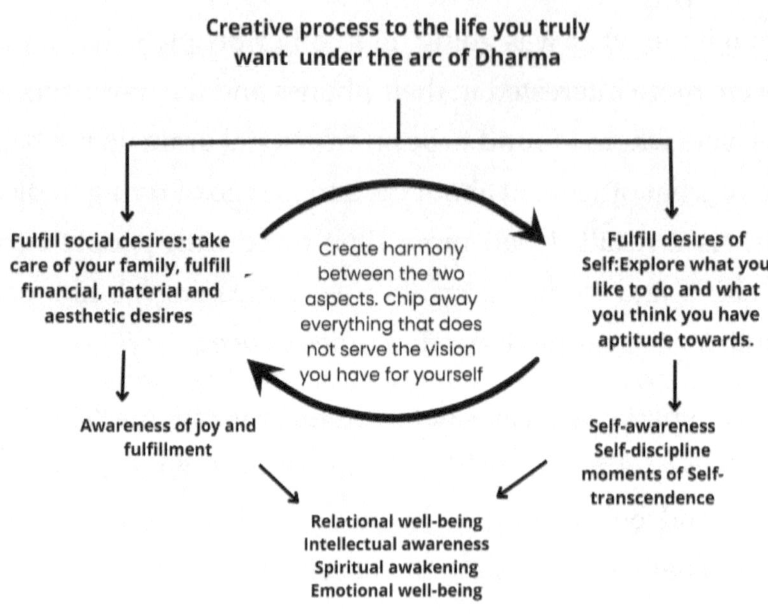

Fig. 12 Creative process

Make no mistake: As easy as the process may seem written on paper, coming into your heartfelt desire and chipping away requires a considerable amount of self-assessment (honest feedback) and a heck of a lot of daring to adapt and evolve as your desires shapeshift (as they do) within a rapidly changing cultural/digital environment.

The path is not easy. You will wonder at times, "Is it worth it?" particularly when you make missteps and others, not so kindly, point out your shortcomings.

It is at such times when you feel yourself spiraling into a dark hole of uncertainty and self-doubts, that you will see a light; a light in the form of a friend who will guide you with a suggestion or an insight, or support you with the resources you need. Their light will transform your life. There will thus be many reasons to celebrate and many moments of soul-felt gratitude. There will be joy like no other when you realize that because you dared to keep going, you became the light for someone. The rays of light will thus shine forth generationally in different shapes and forms. The love, beauty, courage, endurance, hope, empathy, compassion and daring you inspire will verily be your lasting legacy.

R . I . S . E

The people whose stories I tell in this book exemplify a few simple truths: that exploring our desires with interest and curiosity based on what is enjoyable, engaging and enlightening, will make us alive to the moment, that all our "micro" desires will come together to navigate and orient our lives in a particular way toward experiencing heartfelt desires, and that they will give us joy like no other. Whether you come into it with the force of the Ganges River or gradually over a while, when you give voice to your heartfelt desires you are drawn toward courage, compassion, love, daring, intelligence, and strength like you didn't think yourself to be capable. These acts will profoundly transform the relational, intellectual, spiritual, and emotional aspects of your core and outer being.

Let's look at them briefly:

Relational Aspect:

When you take the plunge toward fulfilling your desires, you connect deeply, in more caring and compassionate ways with your spouse/partner, family members and friends. The joy of self-transcendence you will feel in pursuing activities that matter dearly to you will permeate your entire being.

I asked my aunt Kalyani (Parameshwara Rao's wife) what it was like for her to live with a man who was constantly thinking of, or working with the villagers. She said he always discussed the progress and setbacks in the rural development programs with her and sought her counsel. This gave her a sense of participation and more appreciation for his work.

My mother pursued a singing career in addition to her social responsibilities and spending quality time with us. Although it seems counterintuitive, making time for what you truly want to do, opens up time for meaningful and constructive relationships.

Intellectual Aspect:

The term used in Sanskrit for intellect is 'Buddhi.' However, this means more than just intelligence. It means "intuitive discernment" or a deep knowing that comes from the field of soul energy.

As all the stories in this book exemplify, intellectual well-being lights up our lives in different ways:

At the level of learning, the pursuit of any desire is deeply engaging. You will ask questions, seek answers, learn, engage, rethink and relearn in new ways. As a result, you will come up with creative ways of expressing your desires. In the ups and downs of life, you will learn to find ways to know more and do better, as opposed to giving up in frustration.

At the level of decision-making, you will look for solutions from the vantage of your strengths, competence, vision, and skill set.

At the level of your actions and behavior, you will be aware of what motivates you and what your intention is.

At the level of values, your intelligence will help you engage with ideals of truth, love and harmony.

At the level of your emotions, you will engage in identifying the desires that bring joy and determine the right amount of time you can spend on them[48]. The process will help you take off the armor you wear to shield yourself from painful emotions and engage with them proactively.

In all that you do, the harmony you create in your social and spiritual life will help you take the blinkers off your eyes so you can view your reality as is, and see yourself for who you are, rather than who you are supposed to be.

Spiritual Awakening:

Based on my understanding of the essence of the wisdom of seers, I define **spirituality as the recognition that you and I, and the ecosystems around us are inextricably interconnected and interrelated, and held together by the cosmic power that seers characterized as Truth, Unity and Love. Spiritual living is acting and behaving in accordance with these three principles.**

Spiritual awakening is the 'waking up' to the awe-inspiring experience of spiritual living; of seeing yourself within the larger network of human relations and processes and realizing the

48 Tal Ben-Shahar, Happier, Learn the secret to daily joy and lasting fulfillment p.45

magnitude of your "inter-being." Just how deeply every emotion, gesture, and action you express matters to you as well as others. It will make you bow down in humility with a prayer of gratitude for all the beauty, goodness, and joy there is in the world.

You can observe this in your behavior and actions in many ways: when you greet the teller at your local grocery and thank her for her service, when you thank Mother Earth for the food in front of you, when you feel a deep joy in caring for your parents, when you travel to be with a friend whether in grief or in celebration, when tears form in your eyes as you hold a baby and see purity, goodness, and divinity and when in all these experiences you see for yourself an opportunity to examine your own struggles/challenges and positive qualities as a potential resource for moving forward and up.

Spiritual awakening does not mean we become saint-like with no faults. My uncle, about whom you read in the previous segment 'Destiny,' was no saint. He had faults just like the rest of us. But in the power of his heartfelt desire to serve others, his limitations were minimized. What shone brightly was his joy in social activism, the wisdom he saw in the elderly, the love and compassion he felt for his people, and the beauty he saw in the villages. Today, nobody remembers him as an angry, irritable, or unfair person. They remember him as a kind, compassionate leader who grounded his activism upon the teachings of holy scriptures and actions of great leaders before him, and who thus held a light for thousands of villagers to seek their highest destiny.

Emotional Aspect:

When you are connected to your spiritual self, you are emotionally more balanced. When my friend Sanjay was torn between his loyalty to the people who looked up to him and the ideological differences that came up between him and the company, he took time off to look deep within himself and seek what he truly wanted for himself. He did not take any of this as a personal failure but as a standard operating procedure within large organizations. Therefore he was able to cultivate emotional resilience and direct his energies toward positive outcomes.

You experience emotional well-being because you are able to look at failure as an outcome of external factors and not blame yourself, you are able to demonstrate emotional resilience and you are able to channel anger or frustration into positive action.

As you move forward and RISE, here are some suggestions for your consideration:

Befriend your fears

Bringing your desire to life—to give it shape and form is a risky creative process. It involves uncertainties and unknown destinations. In such spaces, fear looms large. Instinctively fear will respond to uncertainties as a threat to your well-being and will try to protect you. Fear will thus draw your attention and warn you of all possible disastrous outcomes. In such situations, if you have been schooled to suppress your fears, they will take control of your life, cripple your self-confidence and highlight all kinds of imaginable, shameful failures.

So I suggest you befriend and appreciate the role of fear in your endeavors. Think of fear as a gentle warning every time you attempt something new and not a harsh critique out to belittle your talents or your capability.

I say this confidently because the book you are holding is a labor of love accompanied by fear—a fear of failure, to be precise. I started by researching the Seer Patañjali, which led to gathering a lot of data on creative living and finally landed on an ancient desire-template. It was a long journey involving the exploration of new and heretofore unknown (for me) ideas. I was afraid I didn't know 'enough.' I was afraid that the response would be 'who is she to write about desires?' Fear churned through my thoughts at every step. So I dug in and enquired further, into texts, into my life and that of others, until I was confident that the words written would serve the larger context of ideas. By the time I started writing, the threat of failure had diminished. Fear had stepped back.

Since then I have thought of the Sanskrit word Abhaya (meaning no fear) not so much as "being fearless" but as having "less fear".

The face of courage, for me, is a soldier's wife whom I met in Myanmar at an Indian Embassy function. I asked her how she dealt with being married to a soldier deployed in high-altitude inhospitable regions, where the risk to life was high. She said she fears and prays for his life every day but if crying and belaboring meant that he left home with a heavy heart, she would look at the bigger picture and find solace in the thought: If soldiers don't protect our country, who will? This is the voice of courage with fear put in its rightful place.

So appreciate the function of fear in your life. It is only doing what it does best—protecting you from imminent danger and keeping you safe. If you recollect, it has been protecting us for more than 70,000 years, when fear enabled us, homo sapiens, to survive, adapt and evolve in every imaginable situation and condition. Befriend your fears and move forward.

Stay rooted to your core values and create strong boundaries

For desires to give us a sense of joy and fulfillment we have to stay rooted to our values and create strong boundaries. In part 1 you listed three core values. Stay with them. Only then will fulfilling desires give you joy and add meaning to your life.

Aligning our values to action is not easy. " Integrity is choosing courage over comfort." It takes courage to stay rooted in our values. When the going gets tough, values will give you the clarity to choose well and guide your actions. Practicing integrity means choosing to check into your values even when you know the odds are stacked against you and forging ahead on your path anyway.

Establishing boundaries for yourself is equally important. How much are you going to be led by other people's opinions? Where do you draw the line and say, 'This isn't working for me, I have to find another way'? We all have a threshold, draw a line and stay within the boundaries.

Be aware of Fate-destiny dynamics

I have known people who blamed fate for their financial predicament rather than take responsibility. To me, observing from close quarters, it seemed convenient to blame forces beyond their control because facing life head-on meant taking ownership and working hard. Fate and destiny are commonly used synonymously and in a casual manner to get oneself off the hook. The problem with this 'fatalistic' viewpoint is that it not only misconstrues the yogic perspective, but also disenfranchises us to actively participate in shaping the life we want and the destiny we should be seeking.

Yogic science, on the other hand, offers an empowering perspective. This is the science of Vedic astrology. According to this science, there is an underlying force to our existence. This underlying force connects us all through a series of actions, thought of as a karmic process. When we 'zoom-in' on our lives we experience this as a force that tugs and pulls us toward some things or some people. They feel like happy coincidences.

We experience this process when we have a sense of déjà vu when witnessing a particular scenario, or when we meet someone and feel strongly that we have met before, when we pick up a book that gives us an answer to the very question we had been thinking about, or when amidst a busy travel schedule, we meet someone at an airport and know instantly he/she is your life partner (this happened to a close friend).

When we 'zoom out' the same force of the Karmic process determines the course of our life, particularly phases of hardships and prosperity. This is the realm of Vedic astrology. However, its determinations are not written in stone. They can be offset by the force of our 'Self-Will'. So if a Vedic astrologer told me I would suffer financial hardships, I can offset that determination by being smart about my finances. It does not mean the astrologer is wrong or that astrology is inaccurate. It simply means I have the power to alter or minimize its effect through my actions.

Linda Johnsen a Vedic astrologer, best articulates this process. She says[49]:

"I've seen numbers of cases where a horoscope reveals that a woman is extremely unlikely to bear a child. Yet after going from one fertility clinic to another, or seeking the blessing of a great saint, she finally conceives. I've also seen charts that show long cycles of financial hardship. Yet through hard work and determination, the individual ultimately creates a comfortable life for himself.

People like these intuitively understand what the yogis have always taught: that destiny is not something that simply happens to you—it's something you actively create through your own thoughts, words, and actions."

The next time, you think you can't help yourself out of a situation, I sincerely hope the power of your Self-Will shows you a way out.

[49] Mapping your Destiny with Vedic Astrology. https://yogainternational.com

Beware of "find your passion" and "be perfect" narratives

As you create boundaries for your integrity practice make sure you don't fall into the trap of 'passion and perfection'.

The much-touted 'find your passion' kicks sand in our eyes. The word passion harbors the illusion that there can be only one thing we can be good at, the sooner we find our 'passion' the happier or more fulfilled we will be. Passion is an outcome of all of our micro desires gathering power and strength as they forge together.

Besides, it is not passion in its singularity, but desires in their plurality that offers a 'range' of positive experiences at every stage of our life. Desire, not passion allows us to explore and experiment with a range of activities and opens a channel for diverse experiences, each adding value to the continuum of our well-being.

Research[50] studies reveal that in a fast-paced, ever-evolving world of hyper-specialties particularly in fields of arts, sciences, and sports, those who desire diverse experience and master interdisciplinary skills are more likely to feel fulfilled than those specializing in one thing. This is because we are innately able to "integrate broadly" with desire as our superpower tool.

Then comes along notions of "Be Perfect."

---

[50] Range: How generalist triumph in a specialized world. David Epstein

Another confounding obstacle that throws us off the desire course is the notion of "perfection." WE have to be perfect and do things perfectly. What does that even mean? Is there a scale to measure? By whose standards should we strive for perfection? The critics or cultural gatekeepers? Striving toward something that doesn't even exist only undermines self-confidence and derails the process of engaging with heartfelt desires.

To fend this off, we have to embrace the practice of strengthening our Will which requires that we acknowledge and focus on our capabilities alone to fulfill our desires. We have to unconditionally accept that we have everything in us to fulfill our desires.

Here's what seers have to say about perfection. I hope it will take a load off your back: **Devotion to and complete engagement with one's duty is the highest perfection**[51].

* * *

After many years of researching, expressing and experiencing my desires, I can say this for sure: it is a hard and brave choice to manifest your desires and it is totally worth all that you chip away to make it happen, for the legacy you create, for the values you inspire and the life you shape for yourself and your loved ones. Exploring your desires and manifesting your heartfelt desire is a battle, that will make you come alive and become the change you always wanted to see in yourself and in others.

As the poet E.E. Cummings rightly said:

---

[51] Bhagavad Gita chapter 8.45-46

"To be nobody-but-yourself-in a world which is doing its best, night and day, to make you everybody but yourself means to fight the hardest battle which any human being can fight, and never stop fighting."

As you dare to give voice to your deepest instincts and move forward in this challenging but most rewarding journey of desire, to paraphrase Obi-Wan Kenobi from the movie Star Wars, **May the force (of desire) be with you.**

REFERENCES

Eknath Easwaran Essence of the Upanishad, A key to Indian Spirituality, 3rd rev.ed., Nilgiri Press 2009, California.

Rajmani Tigunait. The Secret of the Yoga Sutra, SAMADHI PADA. Himalayan Institute. Honesdale, Pennsylvania.2014

Rajmani Tigunait. The Practice of the Yoga Sutra, SADHANA PADA. Himalayan Institute. Honesdale, Pennsylvania. 2017

Eknath Easwaran, The Bhagavad Gita for Daily Living Vol 1-3, Nilgiri Press, 2020, California.

Chinmayananda Swami. Commentary, The Holy Geeta. Central Chinmaya Mission trust. Mumbai. 2008 edition.

Eknath Easwaran, Take your time. How to find Patience, Peace and Meaning. Nilgiri Press, California. 2006.

Tal Ben-Shahar. Happier, Learn the secret to daily joy and lasting fulfillment, McGraw Hill Companies, 2007.

Swamy Mukhyananda: Hinduism, The Eternal Dharma: An evolutionary and Historical perspective.

Gary Zukov. The Seat of the Soul. 25th edition. Simon & Schuster: New York, London, Toronto, Sydney New Delhi.1989.

Gerald James Larson, Ram Shankar Bhattacharya, Encyclopedia of Indian Philosophies Vol. XII, Yoga: India's Philosophy of Meditation. P.30

Brené Brown. Gifts of Imperfection, Hazeldon Publishing, 10th edition 2020. Minnesota

Karen Walrond, The Lightmaker's Manifesto, How to work for change without losing your joy. Broadleaf Books, Minneapolis.

Michael Pollan. This is Your Mind on Plants. Penguin Press, New York, 2021

Kristin Neff and Christopher Germer, The mindful Self-Compassion workbook: A proven way to accept yourself, build inner strength and thrive. Guilford Press: New York, London. 2018.

The Rig Veda. Trans. By Ralph T.H. Griffith.*digireads.com* Publishing. 462 0f 480. Kindle

Paulo Coelho. Alchemist. 25th edition. Trans. By Alan R. Clarke. Harper one. Digital edition, 2021 Kindle.

Mihaly Cikszentmihalyi. Flow: The Psychology of optimal experience.1990. Kindle.

Swami Chinmayananda. Trans Kaṭhopanishad, A Dialogue with Death. Central Chinmaya Mission Trust. 2015

Nelson Mandela. Long Walk to Freedom. Little, Brown and Company. New York, Boston, London.2008 Kindle edition.

Eight Upanishads with commentary of Sankaracharya. Book 2 trans. By Swami Gambhirananda, Advaita Ashrama, Kolkata

M. Monier-Williams. A Sanskrit English Dictionary. edit and revised by Pandit Ishwar Chandra. Parimal Publications.2008

Gerald James Larson, Ram Shankar Bhattacharya. Encyclopedia of Indian Philosophies. Vol XII. Yoga: India's Philosophy of Meditation. Motilal Banarsidass Publishers Private Limited. Delhi. 2nd edition. 2016

Web References:

Atharva Veda hymn 52.

https://www.sacred-texts.com/hin/av/av19052.htm

Brene brown. https://brenebrown.com/resources/atlas-of-the-heart-list-of-emotions/

https://brenebrown.com/wholeheartedinventory/

Bṛhadāraṇyaka Upanishad 4.4.5. *https://www.wisdomlib.org/hinduism/book/the-brihadaranyaka-upanishad/d/doc122058.html*

Rig Veda Book 10 Hymn:129.4. https://www.sacred-texts.com/hin/rigveda/rv10129.htm

The Dialectics of Desire, Joanna Macy, Numen, Aug., 1975, Vol. 22, Fasc. 2 (Aug., 1975), pp. 145-160, Published by: Brill. https://www.jstor.org/stable/3269765

Katha Upanishad 1.2.20.

https://www.wisdomlib.org/hinduism/book/katha-upanishad-shankara-bhashya/d/doc145197.html

Chāndogyopaniṣad 8.1.1

https://www.wisdomlib.org/hinduism/book/chandogya-upanishad-english/d/doc239414.html

Chandogya Upanishad 7.4.2

https://www.wisdomlib.org/hinduism/book/chandogya-upanishad-english/d/doc239349.html

Mundaka Upanishad 3.2.2. *https://www.wisdomlib.org/hinduism/book/mundaka-upanishad-shankara-bhashya/d/doc145134.html*

Śiva Sankalpa Sūtra, chapter 34, verses 1-5, http://www.onlineved.com/yajur-ved/

Kelly McGonigle, How to create a Sankalpa, https://yogainternational.com/article/view/how-to-create-a-sankalpa

Dr. Nayanjeet Choudhury *https://www.RICPHI.org*

Sanjay Rao Chaganti *https://www.sanjaychaganti.com/about-me*

Bhagavatula Charitable Trust. *https://www.bctindia.org*

The Einstein Papers. A Man of Many Parts, by Walter Sullivan, March 29, 1972

https://www.nytimes.com/1972/03/29/archives/the-einstein-papers-a-man-of-many-parts-the-einstein-papers-man-of.html

https://wholebeinginstitute.com

Ganganatha Jha, Manusmriti with the Commentary of Medhatithi
    Verse 6.92

https://www.wisdomlib.org.

Amy Wrzesniewski and Jane E. Dutton. https://positiveorgs.bus.
    umich.edu/wp-content/uploads/Crafting-a-Job_Revisioning-
    Employees.pdf